GHOSTATIŌNS™
THE STORY

by

Bruce Barrymore Halpenny

L'AQUILA

Based on the original **GHOST STATIONS**™ Series (Copyright © 1986)

This New Edition - first published February 2010

British Library Cataloguing in Publication Data
Halpenny, Bruce Barrymore
1. Great Britain. Royal Air Force. Aerodromes. Ghosts.
2. Poetry. Paranormal. Mysteries. Supernatural

ISBN-10: 1-871448-09-3   ISBN-13: 978-1-871448-09-2
L'AQUILA is an imprint of the **ANZIO Group**

Published by:

ANZIO Group
P. O. Box 1212
LINCOLN
Lincolnshire, England
LN5 5LY   www.anzio.co.uk

The Right of Bruce Barrymore Halpenny to be identified as the Author of this Work has been asserted by him in accordance with the Copyright, Designs and Patents Act 1988.

NOTICE: ANZIO Group *does not accept unsolicited manuscripts*

CONTENTS

Grp Capt Max Aitken DSO, DFC, Czech War Cross

COPYRIGHT AND WARNING NOTICE

I get angry with plagiarists because when I was doing my research it was costing me time and money that to this day I have never recouped and I had to make sacrifices, which the plagiarists have never had to. Also no one was interested in the airfields in the 1960's, 1970's and even into the 1980's and many were not even interested about those that had served and their sacrifices. Now everyone wants to jump on the bandwagon but without any of the cost of research or acknowledging those that have made it possible. That is the reason for this and other notices. So …

ACKNOWLEDGEMENTS

My very special thanks to all who have helped me with the books in the **Ghost Stations™ Series** ... those who have talked freely about their ghostly encounters - some for the first time - others who have enriched and filled out old stories in my files. Many, many thanks to all those who have loaned me material and photographs and those who so kindly gave me **exclusive** material and photographs to use as I wished. A special mention for my loyal friend Lord Ancaster; also Peter Tory of the Daily Express and the Daily Mirror who prompted me to use material collected over the years when researching for my books **Action Stations 2** Military Airfields of Lincolnshire and the East Midlands; **Action Stations 4** Military Airfields of Yorkshire; and, **Action Stations 8** Military Airfields of Greater London**,** and write the ghost/mystery book which, with demand from the public for more, became then eight books in the **Ghost Stations™** Series:

Major The Earl of Ancaster, K.C.V.O; T.D; who I enlarge on in the Introduction; John Ainsworth; Allan Allchurch; Mr F.W.E. 'Rik' Appleyard; Richard Allen; Wing Commander H. R. Allen, DFC; Wing Commander David Annand; Mrs. Armstrong (née Bevan); Mr M.J. Arnold; Flight Lieutenant Thomas J. Attrill; Mr R. Austin; Mr P. Avis;

Lord Balfour of Inchrye, PC, MC; Robert A. Bell; Paul Booth; Air Vice-Marshal H. Bird-Wilson, CBE, DSO, DFC, AFC; Mr Ken Billingham; Mrs Ann Binnie; Bob Blunden; Neville Bowles; Mr. J. Brice; Jack Broadhurst; Robert Anthony Brunsdon; Steve

Bond; Mrs Joan Brown; Miss Ruth Baker; Mr P. Bennet; Mrs Bowyer; Louise M. Brazier; Mr B. Brennan; Bob Bryan; Mark Bryan; Mr Bob Ballard; Nicholas Bell; Neville Bower; Flight Lieutenant John Brown; Mr J. R. Bushby; Bundesarchiv, Germany;

Mr D. W. S. Chapman; Mrs June Constable; Mr Bill Corfield; Mr Allan Cram; Peter Crowson; Mr Duncan Currie; Squadron Leader Tony Cunnane; Edward 'Herb' Currotte; Mr John McCaughrean; Courtenay; Mrs Vera Chapple; Norman Carless; Mr A. J. Charlton; Squadron Leader John Cole, MBE, CC; Miss Denise Marie Curran; Mrs Beryl Christiansen, USA; R. Coleman; D. A. Cross; Stuart Chapman; Jim Chatterton; Paul Caputo;

Mr R. C. Daniels; Mr Dennis Davis; Squadron Leader Len Devonshire; Clifford G. Dray; Mr R. Downs; Mr W. Drummond; Dorothy Darwood; Paul Dixon; Mrs Elma Drewry; Wing Commander John H. Dyer; Harry Douse; Ron Day; J. Diamantakos for the Glenn Miller photographs, which were taken by his brother; Betty Dalmond; Mr R. C. Davies; Dennis Davis; David Drew; Squadron Leader Neville Duke, DSO, OBE, DFC; Douglas Durkin; William Deiches - writer and speaker on before Christ History - for permission to quote from the article 'Of Men and Angels'; J.C.Dening; Herr Helmut Dreher, Germany;

Mr. E. A. Easters; J. V. Evans; Mrs Audrey Elcombe; Charles Ekberg; Mrs G. Ettidge; Mark Elliott; Thomas England;

Mrs Alice Farmer; Mr F. Fawke; Mr Bernard Feasey; Squadron Leader Brian Fern; Mr J. L. Fletcher; Robin Fletcher; Syd Frogley; Terrance O'Flynn; Ted Foster; Rosemary Ford; Debbie Francis; Mick Fisher; Captain Laura J. Feldman, The Military Airlift Command, Scott Air Force Base;

Geoff Gardiner; Miss Renee Glynn; Mrs J. Greaves; Mr C. R. Green; Alex Gibson; Colin and Melita Gibson; Peter Giles; Graeme and Janice Garnham; Ralph Gilbert; Stan Galloway; Dr Alan Gauld, Dept. of Psychology, University of Nottingham; Duncan Gray; Mrs Winifred K. Grant; Robert Gray; Mrs Jill Grayson; Janet Gibson; Mrs Joan Goult;

Gareth Hanson; Alan D. Harridence; Mr Derek A. C. Harrison; Mr R. Hawkins; W. Hayes; Mrs Peggy Hayles; Mr Sol Hafeez; Mrs Sheila Heple; Eric Hilton Hewitt; Mr Ian Hogg; Mrs Molly Una Hollis; Stan Holtham; Ex-RAF Sergeant Bernard D. Hughes; Mr E. J. Humphries; Mr Peter Hyde; Bernard Halford; Andrew Hall; Charles Humphrey; Lee Hatfield; Trooper Darryl Hewitt and Carol Hewitt; Geoffrey Hall; Peter Hindley; Mrs Jean Horrocks; Brian Hunter, Rhodesia; Jefrey S. Halik; Mrs Eileen Hodgkins; Heinz von Hahn, Geneve; Werner Hoffmann, Germany; Peter Giles Hull;

Brenda Jackson; Brenda Jenkinson; Mrs R. Jones; Mr E.W. Joyce; Major Robert Keith Jones; Colonel de Jong, Dutch Ministry of Defence; Mr Jack Jones; Ray Jackson; Harry Jury; Alan Jones; Ken Jones; Taffy Jones; Mr & Mrs Jackson;

Mr D. G. Kilvington; Mr G. Kimber; Ian King; Gordon Kinsey; Mr Michael Kelham, MA, Headmaster St. Hugh's School, Woodhall Spa, Lincolnshire; Squadron Leader Ken Kenton; Desmond Keen; Mr J. Keward; Miss Kerry-Leigh Parish, Yeovil;

Mr B. G. Leigh; Ron Lines; Philip Levick; Stephen Lowdon; Gamekeeper Phil Longden; John Langford; Stephen Lewis; Leicester County Council;

Mr Edward (Ted) Marcham; Mrs L.B. McKelvey; Mrs W. Meeson, Wilfred Mills, Mr R.J. Minett; Mrs O. Morton; Neil Mayne; Ministry of Defence, London; Godfrey Mangion, Malta;

Mr E.T. Manby; Mrs Carol Marshall; Martin-Baker Aircraft Co. Ltd; Mrs Moor; Wing Commander Martin; Bob McPhie, Founder The Dodo Bird Club, Canada;

Lorimer Dennis O'Driscoll; Mrs Molly O'Loughlin White; Pete O'Brien;

Mrs Dorothy Pickard; Mr Jock Pepper; Mr Norman Pepper; Miss Prudence Pepper; Mrs C. Petre; Archie R. Pratt; Tom Perrott, Chairman of the Ghost Club, London; Bill Perry; David Peel; Harry Pain; Squadron Leader Colin Pomeroy; Captain R. N. Phillips; David Pearson; Peter Phillips; Charles Plumb;

Captain Barry Radley; Adrian Railton; George Rance; Mr Laurence F. Round; Mrs C.A. Russell; Ernie Reynolds; Squadron Leader Derek Rothery; William Reeves; John (Jack) Riley; Adrian Railton; Mr Raynforth; Mrs Reedman; David Rimmer, Chairman, Clwyd Aviation Group; Mr F.A.C. Roper;

Mrs Joyce Schofield; Mr S. Scott; Mr Chas Selway; Mr V. Simons; Mr W.E. Simpson; Cliff Sims; Norman W.T. Skinner; Mr Gordon Slater; Brian Stafford; Mrs V. Summers; Walt Scott; Carl Schulte, Lausanne; James Silver; Derek Smith; Flying Officer Brian Stephenson VR; Edward Stott; Francis A. Smith; Harry Smith; Miss Margaret Sawyer; Jack Smith; Dave Sutton; Dick Sharphouse; M. Sarson; Werner Schmidt, Germany; Frau Schmidt, Frankfurt-on-Main; Sue Smithson, South Africa; Sheila Staves, Australia;

Mrs Mollie E. Tilley; Mary Tock; Frank Thomas, Western Australia; Jim and Molly Thompson; Les Timms; Mrs Sylvia Tucker; John Turner; Lance Tebbutt; Jan Thorpe; Flying Officer Nicky Tilmouth, WRAF; John W. Tilmouth;

Steven Upton;

Alan Waddington; John Roy Walsh; Mr Paddy Ward; Mr R.F. Warren; Flight Lieutenant John Wears; Mrs Shirley G. Westrup; Harry Willmott; Mike Whalley, Editor, Morecambe Visitor; Mr R. Wilkie; Mr E.W. Winkless; Julia Wolfe-Harlow; Mr Bill Wood; Peter Wright; Keith Wardell; Miss J.A. Wilkinson; Mrs Cella Winstanley; Geoff Whitworth; Denise Williams; Brandon White; William E. Whitehead; Gordon West; Keith Walker; Wilbur Wright; Keith Wright for the poem, photographs and information regarding his brother, Sergeant John Wright; and for permission to publish all of said material.

Jill Yates; Bill and Barbara Young;

I am indebted to the editors of: Air Cadet Journal; Air Force Magazine; Croydon Advertiser Group of Newspapers (G. G. Collard); Daily Mirror - Peter Tory's Diary; Evening Star, Ipswich; Gravesend & Dartford Reporter; Grimsby Evening Telegraph; Lincolnshire Echo; Lincolnshire Standard; Metal Box News - R & D Division Metal Box plc; News of the World (David Gordois); Nottingham Evening Post (Martin Stevenson); Romford Recorder (R. J. Mills); Scottish Daily Recorder & Sunday Mail; Sunday Express (James Kinlay); Sunday Mercury - Birmingham (Peter Mitchell); The Press, Christchurch, New Zealand; Yorkshire Post; Aeroplane Monthly; Airforce Magazine - Canada; Birmingham Mercury; Dodo Club, Station C, Victoria, Canada; Stadtarchive Heilbronn; Die Spiegel; Haller Tagblatt; Flypast Magazine; South Somerset Advertiser; Western Gazette; Western Mail & Echo, for permission to publish the photograph of the haunted restaurant; for their very generous help with request letters, article and permission to quote from published stories. My sincere apologies if I have somewhere quoted from an article or work without acknowledgement, also for photographs. Please contact if one has slipped through my heavy workload.

My special thanks to: Barry J. Goldsmith, who you can read about in: **One Who Writes Poems**; Leon Thompson, USA; Neville Franklin - Control Column; Duncan Blair; Mrs Betty Hockey; Ken Border for his help with some of the research; Robin J. Brooks for West Malling photographs; Denny Densham for the articles and for the **original** tape recordings of the Bircham Newton aerodrome haunting, the **original** tape-recordings of the Bircham Newton update and of the nights investigation at North Weald aerodrome, and for the **original** tape-recordings of the investigation at Borley Church, the most haunted church in the world, and, to use as I wish with all the **original** recordings; Dottore Mario Mignella, Pescara, Italy;

Charlie Chester, Sunday Soapbox Programme; Alex Dickson, Radio Clyde; Keith Skues - Yorkshire Radio Network, Radios Hallam, Viking and Pennine - and Classic Gold Radio; Dennis McCarthy at BBC Radio Nottingham; Hans Plantz for translations; Dave Benfield who sorted out the Glenn Miller photographs; Ted Evans for his military reminiscences and valued help; Mrs Hannah Hunt for the many poems, including 'Breakfast' and 'The long Farewell' with permission to publish as I so wish;

David P. Sandeman, Chairman of The House of Sandeman for permission to reproduce the 'Sandeman Don'; my racing friend Harry Coulby; Walter Laidlaw, Scotland; last but not least, my military friend in Germany, Hermann Laage for great camaraderie. Hermann worked hard on some of the later German stories and some of Hermann's stories have photographic proof, which give you food for thought. See my book: **Ghost Stations™ Germany.**

The material for all the books in the **Ghost Stations™ Series** came from decades of researching and writing about military aviation. Over the years literally thousands of people have contacted me and assisted me; and to everyone … **Thank you.**

The Author and Winco Ken Wallis at RAF Coningsby

INTRODUCTION

One Christmas I got 500 lead soldiers from Santa and these brought many happy hours to a young lad of seven. These are the soldiers I took down to my battlefields in Willingham Woods; and the ones that I mention in my book: **Top Secret RAF Barnham & I**. These taught me many things that stood me in good stead in later life.

I was brought up with the Italian PoWs for my mother was responsible for 15 of them; and it was they who introduce me to pasta. I have eaten spaghetti every day since. Night after night on a summers evening I would watch the RAF bombers from RAF Faldingworth, RAF Binbrook, RAF Wickenby, RAF Scampton, RAF Bardney and RAF Ludford Magna, claw their way into sky, going round and round to gain height.

Former bomber pilot Roger Hoggarth came to teach at Mr Hancock's school in Market Rasen, during my last term there; before - having passed my eleven plus - I went to the De Aston Grammar School in Market Rasen.

The seeds of military interest had been sown. The picture of Johnnie - that I took and show here - was taken in the garden of our Family home 2 Willingham Road, Market Rasen - attached to 101 Squadron at RAF Ludford Magna on Special Duties; and there are no records to show that he served there with RAF Bomber Command. Sadly, he was missing on his 51st Mission; but that is another story.

The other picture shown was also taken in our garden and this shows my father, my uncle George - who had just return from the war in Italy - and myself, holding behind me a .45 pistol that uncle George let me hold. His tales about the war - he was wounded - got me very interested and I spent a great many years researching the war in Italy to produce my book titled: **The War In Italy 1942 - 1945.** Told through eyewitness and first-hand accounts, war diaries written within hours of the events, official documents, reminiscences of Service men and women who survived the war in Italy but also relating the stories of many whose devotion to duty cost them their lives.

This real life drama captures the valour, the hardships and humour. It will give the reader some idea of the men, the machines, the terrain, the elements, the killing, the living conditions, the Italian people … man against man, and friend and foe alike against the elements and the gods of War. The War in Italy 1942 - 1945 is brought alive by the riveting, factual text and the unique photographs that are from my collection and published for the first time. Lord Ancaster was a very loyal and trusting friend; who confided everything with me; even the full facts behind his son. The War in Italy 1942 -

1945 book was just one of my many books that Lord Ancaster and I chewed over at Grimsthorpe Castle, over a damn good meal, wine and a good large cigar.

Lord Ancaster was amazed at the vast amount of research that I had done for the Italy book. I do have many fine photographs with Lord Ancaster, so too Baron; and show just a few here and others elsewhere in this book. One photograph I show of Lord Ancaster laughing, after I had just whispered something military to him and he could not stop laughing. A great man and a great friend, sadly missed; for no such people in 21st century England; oh, better make that Great Britain, for Lord Ancaster had an estate in Scotland, where he went shooting. I love shooting but he could never get me to go with him. Grimsthorpe Castle was only for me; and we certainly had some good laughs, just like the picture you will see of Lord Ancaster in The Air Show chapter.

Brought up on the Blue Books with adventure stories, the comics, Film Fun, Radio Fun, Dandy, Beano, Knockout, Hotspur and the Wizard. These had good stories. All my three brothers served in the army and I served in the Royal Air Force on Special Duties, which included looking after the atomic and chemical weapons; as told in: Top Secret - RAF Barnham & I.

All mysteries fascinate me; very much so military mysteries, and I just have to solve them. A coin has two sides; and for me, there has to be an answer. I am certain that I have solved the mystery surrounding Colonel Thomas Blood; that you will read about in this book; and told here for the first time. No mystery now for my Readers.

During my research … that was vast and actually started in 1946 when I started making notes about all the units and airfields, hence many I speak about with first-hand knowledge.

During this period I interviewed either in person, by letter or by telephone, well over 7,000 people who had served in some branch of the Forces, the most being those connected with the airforce; but also the other United Kingdom Military Forces and Foreign Military Forces. I got over fifteen hundred contacts from my BBC television programme that I did for Mike Derby … see letter from Mike Derby, the Producer.

For my three books in the Action Stations Series I cover in great detail the histories of the airfields for these three books in great depth. My books are:

Action Stations 2 - Military Airfields of Lincolnshire and the East Midlands - with update.

Action Stations 4 - Military Airfields of Yorkshire - with update.

Action Stations 8 - Military Airfields of Greater London - with update.

These three AS books, 2,4,8 are now out of print and all Rights have reverted back to me. **The Copyright ©️ has always been my property and still is.**

BBC

BRITISH BROADCASTING CORPORATION
BROADCASTING CENTRE PEBBLE MILL ROAD BIRMINGHAM B5 7QQ
TELEPHONE AND TELEGRAMS 021-472 5353

2nd March, 1983.

Bruce Barrymore Halpenny, Esq.,

Dear Barry,

Please find enclosed some
more letters about "To Shatter the Sky",
some from your friends I think!

Your may be interested to know
that 0.8 million people watched the
programme, which was the largest audience
for a regional programme on that night.
78% of the people who watched it enjoyed
the programme which is very good.

I have passed the programme to
BBC Leeds, and they may run it there at a
later date.

Yours sincerely,

Mike Derby
PRODUCER
RTV Midlands

17

As stated, I did a vast amount of research, the bulk of which was only available due to my Special Duties in the RAF Military Police. RAFPD Provost. That opened many doors that only I could open. In my interviews were many ghostly stories and stories of the supernatural, which I put into special files; and these, grew and grew.

One day, Peter Tory, then with the Daily Express running the William Hickey column; asked me what I was doing with all the ghost stories. He said everybody loves a ghostie story. I said done nothing and he then said he would see what the public thought via his page. He did so and from that came **Ghost Stations™ 1**. It was an instant hit and from **Ghost Stations™ 1** came a flood of material; that gave **Ghost Stations™ 2, 3, 4, 5, 6, 7 and 8.** It was very nice but very, very hard work to keep pace with public demand.

I have a vast amount of material that still needs sorting; and this includes poems and photographs; and thank all who have been kind enough to send to me.

I am working on a poem book; but have put that on hold for the moment; and from my said poem book, I include in Ghost Stations™ The Story a section from my Elucidation Chapter; that makes clear the meaning of poetry in the chapter: One Who Writes Poems. I am certain that you will find it very interesting. I also include some of my poems in this book; one being a lovely poem written by Nancy Robins when she was 14 years old; who on sending the poem signed the letter in December 1990, Mrs Nancy O'Brien. Nancy goes on to say: *"I am sending a photo of myself aged 13 years with my younger brother and sister. It was taken in Liverpool in 1940. You can just see the edge of our air raid shelter behind us.*

" I was sent to live with relations in Mancot, (Sealand airfield was about 2 miles away.) I stayed there for about one year, from the end of 1940 to the end of 1941.

"The school I attended was Deeside Selective Central School, Shotton, Chester. We were asked to write a patriotic poem for an EISTEDDFOD. I don't know if it was just our school, or if others were involved. I hope this information is enough for you.

"We have managed to get one of your books from the library 'Action Stations', my husband is reading it. I think the photos are exceptional. I was a telephonist in the W.A.A.F from 14.2.46 to 11.2.48. My first posting was Tangmere my last Kirkham. Would you let me know when your new book will be available.

"Yours sincerely, Nancy O'Brien."

Well Nancy, it will be available in February 2010, for your poem will be in this book; under the title: A Patriotic Poem, and will follow straight after the Introduction. The other poems, one after Nancy's and the others after: One Who Writes Poems. The last poem in the book being; Knights of The Round Table, for on the first line of my Introduction I mention 500 lead soldiers. So the poem to end with just had to be Knights of The Round Table. I am sure you will agree.

Now my good Fans, you will have noted that the children were asked to write a patriotic poem … Those were the Good Old Days when Patriotism was not a dirty word; and Pride of One's Country and Common Sense prevailed.

Oh, Nancy said: *"One light evening I was in the bedroom and heard the sound of heavy planes engine, very low. Watching out of the window I could see it was a German plane. All of a sudden a Spitfire zoomed into view, flew around the German plane, and brought it down.*

"Shortly after, we were asked to make a patriotic poem for the school eisteddfod. The enclosed poem came to mind and it came in first. Hope you like it." Signed Mrs Nancy O'Brien.

As stated, you can read Nancy's poem after the Introduction.

It was a great pleasure to supply my material to HMV from my story **'Through The Viewfinder'** in **Ghost Stations™3;** and it is now in their archives. I said to HMV that I would gladly help if they sent a picture of Nipper … that they quickly did and it is in pride of place; along with Air Dog Blaze, Toby and Bruce.

Mine are **true** ghost stories; and proof - if proof were needed - that there are ghosts; one has only to take the story of the American Phantoms at RAF Kimbolton, told in **Ghost Stations™ 1**. Corporal Warwick gives

Number 8 Flight a verbal lashing and threats that there were no ghosts present. The very next evening after sighting the Phantom American airmen and the ghostly B-17 Flying Fortress on the airfield, he was the third one to be admitted to Station Sick Quarters.

As stated, mine are true stories; and if you see any of ANZIO text or photographs published in any publications or displayed anywhere without an ANZIO License number to publish or display our material … that is piracy.

Only ANZIO can issue a License.

Neither ANZIO nor I as the Author have anything to do with the ALCS - Authors' Licensing & Collecting Society.

So please get in touch with ANZIO and give where, what and when you saw it. Any damages ANZIO gets will be shared fifty-fifty after costs.

On page 146 in Ghost Stations™ Lincolnshire I say on the last two lines of the story about The Runway Ghost at RAF Binbrook; that: The proof of what I say will be made clear in Ghost Stations™ The Story. So let me now do so.

The Sergeant was killed on the runway when the Wellington bomber was just getting airborne and just about passing over the Sergeant who had run down the runway waving for the bomber to abort the take-off; but he was too late. The Wellington bomber exploded overhead, killing the Sergeant Armourer.

I say in the story that the Sergeant Armourer thought that the bombs had been armed when loaded into the bomber; and in a desperate attempt to stop the bomber getting airborne he had chased down the runway. The facts are that the bomb or bombs exploded owing to incorrect positioning of safety devices.

So there you have it. The biggest problem was hang-ups due to icing; and that was not only during the war; but also many times in the early Fifties with the Canberra when at Binbrook, Scampton and Marham.

I do also say in my book: TOP SECRET RAF BARNHAM & I on page 78; that I do have a photograph of Toby with his 'cigar' and will see if I can find it for the reprint. Well, I have found the photograph and will publish it in this book first. So just look at Toby with his cigar. He had just seen me light up one of my cigars,

Toby with his "cigar"

that being a King Edward Invincible from the Americans, and minutes later as I turned round, there stood Toby with his cigar. I had to laugh and took the photograph that you now see.

A special mention to all my many Fans who send me e-mails and letters. Thank you one and all; and to you Ingrid Craig Conway, who met me in a Lincolnshire market town on 5th January 2009. I was talking to my dear friend Jean Staves and Ingrid, excitedly introduced herself as a big fan of Ghost Stations™, and wanted to know when more would be out. Well, here is one.

Bruce Barrymore Halpenny
Roma
Italia

February 2010

The Barrymore Halpenny Family on a Special visit to the Battle of Britain Flight at RAF Coningsby. Left to Right: Marian, Baron and the Author, Bruce Barrymore Halpenny.

23

A PATRIOTIC POEM

One night in an air raid when it was still light,
I saw one of our Spitfires put up a grand fight.
It flew round a Heinkel; it flew round with ease,
And soon had the Heinkel down among the trees.
So there you see, no wonder we brag,
They can't bring down the British Flag.

BLESS 'EM ALL

Several years ago now my holiday was spent,
Travelling up in Lincolnshire with my old bike and my tent.
I'd been cycling round the countryside the best part of a week,
Looking for old airfields, abandoned now and bleak.

It was on the Friday evening as the sun was going down,
That I jumped upon my bicycle and headed out of town.
The air was warm and still that evening and I was rather dry,
"The next pub that I come to, I'll have a pint," said I.

I was right out in the country now away from all the din,
When down a narrow winding lane, I came upon an Inn.
It seemed to be quite popular judging by the cars,
And the sound of happy voices that came from both its bars.

I had found an ancient tavern; it was called The Cunning Fox,
And inside all around the place were lots of antique clocks.
There was one I saw, it caught my eye as it hung there on the
wall,
And underneath, a photograph, with these words, 'BLESS 'EM
ALL'.

The photo showed an aircraft, a Halifax no less,
There was something in the way it stood that really did impress.
I was looking closely at it when someone tugged my sleeve,
I turned, and found an old man, about seventy I believe.

He looked at me with eyes aglow and waved a gnarled hand,
"I knew the boys who flew in her, by gum lad they were grand."
He smiled at me, "Sit down," he said, and showed his empty glass,
"Stay here," I said, "I'll get a drink if these will let me pass."

I fought my way up to the bar and ordered him a beer,
The Landlord, handing me my change, said, "You're a stranger here."
I told him I was touring, old airfields for to see,
He said he knew of one or two, or was it two or three.

With glass held high I elbowed through that noisy happy throng,
But when I reached my seat again, the old man he had gone.
There was no way he could have left; the bar had just one door,
And that was on the other side, I'd have seen him there I'm sure.

Just then up came the Landlord wiping tables down,
"Something wrong?" he asked me when he saw my puzzled frown.
I told him of the old man whose eyes were all aglow,
The Landlord leaned across and said, "I think you've seen our Joe."

"An interesting story is what I have to tell,
I'll talk to you when I've closed up, you can stay the night as well."
I thanked him for his offer and said I'd like to hear,
His interesting story, then sat down to drink my beer.

The crowd inside the bar now began to peter out,
The Landlord rang the old brass bell; "Last Orders!" came the shout.
Eventually the pub was closed, all was peaceful, quiet and still,
And the Landlord draped an old bar towel across the silent till.

He poured out two large whiskeys; I noticed both were neat,
"Come and meet the wife," he said, "And have a bite to eat."
He told her what had happened down in the bar below,
At once she raised her hand and said, "I know, he's seen our
Joe."

Over sandwiches and coffee the Landlord told me all,
About old Joe, the photo, and the clock upon the wall.
Now to put you in the picture the best thing I can do,
Is tell you what he said to me, and believe me it's all true.

Two or three miles up the road back in 1943,
There used to be an airfield, the old Mess you still can see.
Halifax and Lancaster flew from there each night,
And to see those aircraft taking off believe me was a sight

One aircraft I should mention, a Halifax Mk.2,
Had flown on many missions and was cherished by her crew.
'BLESS 'EM ALL', they called her, and proud they were to show,
Her name in letters on the nose, they had named her after Joe.

Joe had a small allotment quite near the runways end,
And all day long he worked at it and watched the planes ascend.
He would stand in awe and wonder, as every plane took off,
Murmuring softly, "Bless 'Em all," and his old flat cap he'd doff.

Old Joe was quite a character, and that one Halifax crew,
Adopted him as their mascot, which thrilled him through and
through.
In the evenings when not flying, at the Fox they'd buy him beer,
And they'd laugh and pat his tired old back, as he made it
disappear.

Now Joe was in his seventies, a perky chap, quite small,
And at The Cunning Fox he'd sit near the clock upon the wall.
It seems the ticking pleased him; it had a soothing sound,
Until one night a drunken airman knocked the old clock down.

Without his well-loved timepiece old Joe became depressed,
And this upset his favourite crew; they no longer flew their best.
Then their skipper had an idea that he thought might put things right,
They'd collect old Joe and take him to the Mess that very night.

They feasted him right royally; he nearly swam in beer,
And they noticed how he kept his eyes upon the fireplace near.
Upon the ledge above the fire there stood a fine old clock,
And Joe's old head kept nodding to its comforting tick-tock.

Then it was time the skipper said, to take their old friend back,
And some of the men slipped cigarettes into the pockets of his mac.
The C.O. of the station stood up and raised his hand,
"There is something I should like to do for one we think so grand."

Saying this he reached up and took the clock from off the shelf,
"Here Joe, you have it, you keep it for yourself."
Joe's eyes began to water; he knew not what to say,
He clasped it to his beer-stained coat as they cheered him on his way.

Next evening at The Cunning Fox old Joe stood six feet tall,
He proudly showed his nice new clock then hung it on the wall.
He would wind it, he would dust it, and I'm very pleased to say,
No Landlord's ever moved it; it's on that wall to stay.

Now the photo underneath the clock, Joe's clock upon the wall,
Was presented to the Landlord by the crew of BLESS 'EM ALL.
It shows their well-loved Halifax just before they went to Kiel,
And if you look you'll see old Joe beside the starboard wheel.

Two missions later they took off and climbed into the blue,
That also was the evening old Joe last saw his crew.
By six the following morning the surviving planes returned,
But of BLESS 'EM ALL there was no sign, the ground-crews
stomachs churned.

They stood around in little groups with hands up to their eyes,
Listening for that familiar sound as they slowly searched the
skies.
They hoped, they prayed, they would not believe that fate had
cast the dice,
There wasn't one among them who believed they'd paid the
price.

Someone asked, "Who'll tell old Joe? He'll be shattered I'll be
bound,"
When far away they heard it, a faltering engines sound.
Now Joe on his allotment also heard this ghastly noise,
But he didn't know that aircraft was the one that held his boys.

Then at last they saw it far away across the trees,
And what they saw made each airman tremble at the knees.
One engine was not working as far as they could tell,
But what was worse a bomb was lodged beneath the plane as
well.

All knew that it was BLESS 'EM ALL and they held their breath and froze,
But they couldn't see its name because the plane had lost its nose.
The brave survivors of its crew had battled to get home,
For mile on mile they'd struggled to try to reach their drome.

The tower tried to call them but their radio was out,
They didn't know the bomb was jammed beneath the plane, no doubt.
For if they had I'm sure they would have tried to work it free,
And ditch it somewhere safely as they flew across the sea.

The aircraft made a circuit, then came in low to land,
The Ambulance and Fire Tender standing close at hand.
It wasn't going to make it everyone could feel,
For when the undercart came down, it had also lost a wheel.

Lower ever lower; it made its fateful pass,
It didn't hit the runway but pancaked on the grass.
The bomb beneath the Halifax went off with deafening roar,
And blasted into nothing BLESS 'EM ALL for evermore.

Thick acrid smoke then billowed up as bits of wreckage fell,
Then they found Joe on his allotment, killed by the blast as well.
Now no one can forget the time Joe and his boys got chopped,
For that's the time when old Joe's clock gave up the ghost and stopped.

At 8.15 precisely that old clock's hands were stilled,
It seemed as if it knew exactly when its friends were killed.
And sometimes like tonight for instance old Joe pays a call,
And sits beneath his favourite clock and photo on the wall.

So ends the Landlord's story, though sad it seems to be,
But I hadn't bargained for the shock that was going to come to me.
I had stayed on at The Cunning Fox most of the following day,
And early in the evening I once more cycled on my way.

I found that wartime airfield that the Landlord talked about,
And saw the one-time Mess with its windows all knocked out.
I decided then and there that in those ruins I would camp,
I knew that in these parts it could get very cold and damp.

I settled down inside its walls and lit a cheery fire,
And round about eleven I decided to retire.
I cannot say when I awoke but I found myself alert,
As a bright light lit up the room, it was so strong it hurt.

Then far across that Mess-Room in that bright lights eerie glow,
I counted seven aircrew, and the eighth one was old Joe.
Among his aircrew buddies he stood there straight and tall,
He turned and smiled and proudly said, "They're my lads, Bless 'Em all."

SO WHAT IS FOLK-LORE?

The term Folk-lore refers to the lore (knowledge) of the folk (people) surviving in living tradition, and not acquired from books. The term Folk-lore was first used by William J. Thoms in his book Atheneum of 25 August 1846, as a collective name for traditional Literature, customs, ghost stories and superstitions found among the peasantry of civilized countries. Thoms was the founder of Notes and Queries in 1849, and he edited it till 1872. Thoms was also the author of books on early romances, lays and legends.

The earliest writer who, like myself, set himself the mammoth task to collect folk-lore was John Aubrey (1626 - 1697) the antiquary, one of the first members of the Royal Society.

I was the first person to have published the Ghost Stations™ Series that covered true ghost and mystery stories from military bases and all other airfields. It took a lot of time and a hell of a lot of money and hard Work; and no plagiarists are going to steal my Work and think they can get away with it … see © Copyright and Warning Notice. Like my research for the Ghost Stations™ Series of books, the Brothers Grimm collection was the earliest collection formed on the scientific principle of setting down what they heard exactly as they heard it, without embellishment, addition or omission. In 1822 an issue of a volume completed Brothers Grimm Work.

Like mine, in the main, this principal for my ghost and mystery stories was faithfully adhered to, hence the Bruce Barrymore Halpenny True Ghost Mystery stories.

K. and W.K. Grimm made collections of Marchen (published 1812 - 1815) and showed that these had not only a psychological but historical value. They adopted the view that Teutonic, Greek, and Indian myths were of Indo-European origin. Mannhardt (1865) paid special attention to the lore associated with the agricultural mode of life surviving among peasants, and found traces of an ancient pagan religious system that had been supplanted by Christianity. His views, especially in connection with vegetation deities, strongly influenced later writers.

There are few of the beliefs and observances traditional among the peasantry of Europe, which are not traceable to a religious source, or at least to originals which bear a deep religious imprint. The annual procession and legend of Lady Godiva have been traced to a religious ceremony practised by the ancient Britons.

For me the best mythologies are the Greek, Roman, and Norse. Now, it is possible that these mythologies, have stories in common; for example, that of the flood and the re-peopling of the world; then the task of the mythologist becomes much more interesting, for he has to decide whether such an event took place or whether borrowed from the legends of one race into those of another.

Ancient mythology is all around you in your daily life; for certain days of the week are named after the chief deities of the Norse mythology - Wednesday is Wodin's day and Thursday is Thor's day; the fifth day of the week, so called from the old Teutonic god of thunder, Thor. Yule-tide log, the celebration of Easter, and many other festivals are based on ancient pagan practices. Early Christian missionaries quickly adopted many heathen feasts and deities, giving them Christian characteristics and interpretations. The Atlas Mountains in North Africa got their name from the ancient god, Atlas, who held up the heavens on his shoulders - the mountains, being cloud topped, seem to reach to the sky. The constellations of the sky were all explained by reference to the ascension of heroes to heaven; Castor and Pollux - or the Gemini - were half-mortal heroes who were placed in the sky at their passing; Venus and Jupiter were the brightest planets in the firmament; Diana or Cynthia, the chaste goddess, was the cold moon; and Orion's belt and the Pleiades were similarly explained.

Although stories containing mythological elements are now all most a thing of the past and only a few still linger. In the customs associated with Christmas, New Year's Day, Easter, May Day, and Hallowe'en are some of great antiquity. Charms, mascots and such are still worn for 'Good Luck,' which in ancient times meant everything desired by man, including good health, longevity, good fortune, offspring, and happiness.

Mythology is the scientific investigation of traditional beliefs; also the aggregation of such beliefs or myths. The word myth originally simply meant speech, then in a narrower sense, a tale or tradition, particularly one handed down from prehistoric times giving, in the form of a story about a god or a hero, some ancient belief regarding the processes of nature, customs, or problems of cosmogony. Mythology means in the first place, the whole body of the myths of a particular country, or circling round a particular figure, as when we talk of Greek or Norse mythology; in the second place, mythology is the scientific study of myths, their analysis and explanation. While mythology deals largely with questions of Gods and the origins of things, religion is only one aspect of it. The mythologies of many lands, for example, contain a story of a deluge, but it has not always a religious significance, and is often simply cosmogonic, that is, purely scientific or even historical. The religious view of Zeus as the chief of the immortals who dwelt of Olympus, is very different from the mythological view, which has also to account for the stories of his amours in the form of animals, and many other myths which one is surprised to find in circulation among so cultured a people as the ancient Greeks. Myths are largely answers to questions propounded by uncivilized man; and all peoples seem to have speculated on the origin of the world and man.

WARTIME MEMORIES

Betty Hockey has many memories from those far off wartime days. Betty and her Nonstops Troop Show gave over 1,000 concert shows to forces under Southern Command and, they did a marvellous job during those dark days. Betty had a daytime war job of driving a van around the area, collecting used tyres for recycling. Thus she was able to call into any camp or unit to ask if they would like the show to visit them. Needless to say they never refused. Indeed, once having been, there was always a great demand for them to return. The 'Nonstops' were very popular with all those in uniform.

The 394th Bomb Group United States Air Force was stationed at Holmsley South Airfield just prior to D-Day. Basically it was RAF and Betty made arrangements to give their show out there on the eve of D-Day. "Little did we know what was to happen that night," said Betty. "All hell let loose I guess."

There was a marquee erected for the show and they were warned that there would be much comings and goings. For this reason they sang the National Anthem and the Star Spangled Banner before the show instead of after as was usual.

"There was much tension in the air and one sensed that something awful was about to happen yet not knowing what," said Betty. "The Anthem went off uninterrupted, as usual with the British.

"We started the Star Spangled Banner to sing intentionally just one verse as usual, as a gesture to the GIs, we managed to get almost through it when it was taken right out of our hands by around 400 voices in unison and they sang that as if that was to be their last. As indeed it was, for some of them.

"We all just stood on stage absolutely helpless. The tears streamed down all our faces and so did they in the audience. Most of those boys were only kids. I am afraid I cannot, I just cannot; go out on that airfield now without I hearing that singing ringing in my ears. It's eerie."

Betty Hockey was taken out there just prior to the D-Day anniversary in 1984 to do a film for both BBC and also the American NBC.

"Each time I could hear those voices and the roar of the planes as they took off," said Betty. "That airfield is now in disuse and hardly anything of those years visible, yet those two visits brought it all flooding back. I often wonder just how many of those boys came back. If they didn't, did they go out with some of the songs of our show on their lips? I would like to think so. I would like to think that we played a very, very tiny part in raising their morale before they left."

Was this the 'Ghostly Music' heard by Helen Bevan and Valerie Sager? Or, was it 'The Missouri Waltz' heard by Derek Harrison? Or was it the Americans singing that Mrs Christine Russell heard, 'The Phantom Party at Odstock Maternity Hospital'?

All camps were 'sealed' just prior to D-Day so, instead of the usual travelling to the camp and going in, being expected, Betty Hockey and the Nonstops were told that they had to rendezvous with a motor-cycle escort, (they were not supposed to know where they were going), which was a farce as Betty had previously visited said camp to book the show.

"However, it was no hardship to meet at the local pub - the very old Cat and Fiddle," said Betty. "From there - well oiled - we were escorted into the camp. But,

Betty, The Can-Can Dancer

laugh upon laugh, with the motor-cycle escort and me driving our leading car of four, we promptly turned off into a side road remembering that the rest of our cars behind were dotted in and out the army convoy which we had encountered on the road.

"You can well imagine the utter confusion that evolved when this convoy, together with the rest of our cars, got stuck in this very narrow lane.

So did we. There was utter chaos as each army vehicle, including tanks, had slowly and surely to back up, back on to the main road again. You see, it was dark, very dark, and they had followed **my** car, which was an old Canadian Army staff car - a big Ford V8 painted in its khaki colour. However, we made it and the show went on."

Another base visited by Betty Hockey and her Nonstops was at Ringstead Bay in Dorset. It was the living quarters area of the RAF camp and airfield that was at nearby Warmwell. They had been there many times. Then suddenly, without warning to Betty it was turned into an American 'All Blacks' camp. "I must admit that they were a very good audience and gave us a wonderful welcome," said Betty. "But one could not help noticing that the treatment and respect of them was not good by the white Americans. However, that situation has improved enormously now."

Then, the next time they went to Ringstead they noted barbed wire all around. Nothing daunted, in they went as by this time they had learned not to be surprised by anything. The Commanding Officer let them unload all their scenery and props, and **then** he told them that it was now a German prisoner of war camp.

"Right, everything back on the trailer," said Betty. "Were they not our enemy?" But the Commanding Officer asked as a special favour to him that they give the show. He told them that they were a grand bunch of fellows. "As indeed we found out," said Betty - "but it did go against the grain." They were given an interpreter and the show went well with much appreciation from the Germans. Needless to say, Betty and her troupe kept that all very quiet and never let on to a soul until around three years ago. The Commanding Officer also asked for a further special favour, that of leaving their props and scenery behind so that the PoWs may have an outing the next day by bringing it all back on a huge truck. They were under guard, so all went well.

"I still have photos of those men unloading and now, of course, would dearly like to put names to those faces," recalls Betty. "Because of this episode, I was invited by the Deputy Chief of German Army Staff to visit a German Regiment in 1983 and spent two whole days with them in barracks staying with the Commandant and his wife. They were two charming people and my life is richer for having met them all."

Beaulieu Airfield in Hampshire was another place they visited and believe it or not, it was the only place where they could 'win' some petrol with which to keep their cars on the road to do the shows. Betty had no difficulty in booking the concert party up, especially for the small camps, or units, which were under canvas and never saw any sort of entertainment. So, each time she was around Beaulieu she carried a large empty carboy, which normally contained distilled water. Then it was arranged that the carboy would quickly be filled with petrol. "No doubt aviation fuel as it stank to high heaven," said Betty. "I well remember pulling out on to the road right in front of a police car. Whew!

"I had a few moments of panic. The fuel absolutely reeked so naturally I had the windows open. I quickly shut them and nearly gassed myself but I was certain that they must have got scent of me. However, they followed on for about ten or so miles when I suddenly had an idea and quickly pulled into a farm which I knew, and knowing the farmer would co-operate, he very swiftly yanked out the carboy and closed the doors. A hairy moment. I need not have worried, the police car just merely went on its way."

"Stoney Cross Airfield in Hampshire was a joy to visit and an American base where food was plentiful. At that airfield the men would patrol around Bournemouth in jeeps just literally waiting to 'kidnap' girls right off the street. And this they did very efficiently. The girls would soon find themselves at the dance hall on the station. And they sure gave them a good evening. When the 'Nonstops' had finished their shows they were always entertained in the Officers' Mess.

"High jinks too, and at that particular base it was an every time occurrence to pile on to jeeps and try to chase the taking off planes on a race to the end of the airfield," recalls Betty. "Crazy days, but happy ones. Guess only the Yanks were capable of such antics."

Another of the many airfields visited by Betty and her troupe was RAF Netheravon in Wiltshire. This was an old airfield dating back to before the First World War; and you can read about it and see the only known photographs of the airfield that I took, for my book: Top Secret RAF Barnham & I.

When Betty's petrol supply ran out or maybe tyres too bad to travel; they always had the option of asking the camp to send out a 10-ton truck, or Betty could always hire a coach and Southern Command would pay the bill. In one case they asked for a 10-ton truck, which was duly sent with a black American driver.

"Goodness, was that guy crazy," said Betty. "He drove like a maniac, mounting kerbs, etc. and generally enjoying himself. But, the considerate Entertainments Officer had put in 16 NAAFI type easy chairs, which sadly to say were on castors. We spent the whole journey like being on a roller coaster and no way could we attract the driver's attention in the cab. Needless to say we refused to be transported home that way, as we were literally black and blue. They sent us home in a series of Staff cars."

Betty added: "I have often wondered just how many of those wonderful boys that we played to returned. Did they go out of this world humming one of the tunes they last heard of at our Concert Party? - I would like to think so. I cannot now ever go out on an airfield without tears in my eyes, and, without that crescendo of voices haunting in my ears. It seems just as if it were yesterday."

Captions for photographs pages 43 and 44.

Betty Hockey in 1944 in her Training Corps Uniform; and on page 44 we see Betty in 1990 in the same wartime uniform – and just as lovely – after I requested her in said uniform for in my book Wartime Poems.

THE NONSTOPS TROOP SHOW

TIP-TOP
VARIETY
SUN. NOV 5.
1944.
VELMORE
CAMP
CHANDLERS FORD.

So, let me now tell you more about Betty and The Nonstops Troop Show in their own right; and, I am certain you will be interested, for they did a damn good job and the troops were always pleased to see them.

The Nonstops Troop Show performed five nights a week; and it was a very hard task to do so for all the Artistes had a full-time day job of some sort of War Work. The Nonstops gave well over a thousand voluntary Shows in the Southern Command area and travelled within a forty-mile radius of Bournemouth each time.

When they visited Units as a complete party, there were 16 Artistes, Peggy the Soprano was an Officer in the American Red Cross; Sandy, a much lined old Fisherman, sleight of hand; Billy, the Comedian who ran a Transport Café; Dippy, a soldier stationed in Bournemouth; Gus, a Cartoon Artist; Pat, Baritone was in building; Iris and Norman, a man and wife act on vibes and accordion; Nellie, a Nellie Wallace type

45

comedian; Betty – who you have just read about in the previous chapter – was the Principal Dancer doing Can-Can, Hula, Seven Ceils and so on; Peggy on the piano; Mac, electrician; the three dancers, Monica, Pat and Babs; and finally Ken, dressed in an evening suit and sporting a monocle, was the Compere

They travelled in a convoy of four cars; and with the assistance of the local Motor Pool – volunteer cars and drivers – they were able to keep going without too many transport difficulties, although petrol supplies proved a problem. An allocation was made for a certain amount, which by no means covered their needs. With an odd can or two from Units they managed fairly well until they became so popular and demands upon them became greater. Betty, their leader contacted the Petroleum Board, but the claim was refused. Notwithstanding she promptly made a personal call upon the reading Office, but she had no joy there, so armed with a name she proceeded to Mill Bank in London, but had pressure in getting to the "name". Having gone to that much trouble Betty was not to be daunted and sat upon the floor and refused to move. Clearly somebody had to take action – she was seen – and the result was a further two gallons of petrol per car. It was a big help and saved the day.

The Nonstops ran four different shows thereby enabling them to return to any Unit within one week if requested. The first half was a variety show with each artist doing a single spot. The second half was run as a revue and very popular these second halves were.

Hula-Hula girls, Betty and Babs.

The first show was a South Sea skit with Hula-Hula girls. The second was a typical Parisian Café show with Can-Can. The third show was a Western and the fourth was Eastern.

Needless to say, that all were extremely very popular; especially as they included audience participation. No need to elaborate it was not difficult to get volunteers on stage.

Each Artiste loved the work and were always willing to turn out with just a few hours notice as indeed they did many times when the Prisoners of War returned from Japan. These lads were in a dreadful state and the

Nonstops were privileged to be amongst the first white women the PoW's had seen for a long time.

They were a pitiful sight; how could the Party refuse when requested to visit, sometimes five nights in a row? The memories of those Boys haunt even to this day – January 2010 – some with front teeth missing from blows by the buts of rifles. They arrived on the Queen Mary at Southampton and were taken to the Transit Camp, which was on Southampton Common.

It was a joy to play to such wonderful people and they were so appreciative. The memories of those PoW's were unforgettable; especially as German PoW's were there to wait upon their needs. Need anything more be said?

The Nonstops pause for a photo call.

Silly stories come to mind when thinking of various Camps and Units in those dark days, which did much in fact to relieve tensions. Such things as girls walking along pavements, being 'kidnapped' and whisked off in jeeps only to find themselves at a dance or party at some Airfield or Camp. Who would be responsible for such carryings on? The Americans of course. It was all good harmless fun. The favourite game was to pile the girls into jeeps and chase the taking off aeroplane across the airfield, in an effort to race them to take-off. Dangerous it no doubt was; but again harmless fun.

Betty recalls a visit to Verne Citadel at Portland where they went many times. Upon leaving the Mess after a party, which inevitably followed a Show, one of the cars refused to start. The artistes were piled into the three remaining cars to go home whist Betty stayed behind for the night, having been provided with a camp bed in the Sergeant Major's children's room. This Sergeant Major was a wonderful person, much liked and adored by the men, in spite of his control on the Parade Ground. His attitude was: "You may break your Mother's heart, but you will not break mine." He was a kind man and a true friend to any soldier who needed help. He only had one arm and his name was Ticky. Betty will never forget this person and his charming wife.

It seemed the middle of the night when Betty was awoken at six a.m. and told to get dressed. One did not stop to question the orders of such a person, as one always knew there was reason for such an order.

Betty arose and dressed as requested then strode across the Parade Ground at his side wondering the reason for such an early morning walk. He said: "I want you to see a wonderful sight." Then peering down the steep cliffs, amongst the swirling mist and fog, emerged the vision of many Battleships and Destroyers. "What a moment that was," said Betty "A feeling of such safety and power of those ships, to think that they were guarding us and our shores." It was sight she would never forget; and indeed, she never has.

Verne has now reverted to the prison it formerly was. Betty was sorry not to have been able to revisit the place that was perhaps the Nonstops favourite Camp of the war. Betty recalls the problems.

"When visiting a camp under canvas and wallowing in mud in the New Forest just prior to D-Day we had to meet up with a motor-cycle escort to be taken to said Camp," said Betty. "It was truly farcical, as I had already visited this Camp to arrange the Show and knew exactly where it was and which Unit etcetera. However, as all the Camps prior to D-Day were known as 'sealed Camps' this was the ruling.

"Because of meeting the escort, the Show arrived late and were rushed to the Dressing Room. The Unit had gone to considerable trouble in using a large Army tent for the Concert, with a stage built at one end which we had to climb up and go over into a Dressing Room made of another smaller tent completely laced on to the large one. All very nice and compact. But, where were the toilet facilities? The Entertainment Officer's face fell when he

realised that he had not thought of such a thing. So red faced away he went.

"Incidentally the flooring on the Dressing Room was just a tarpaulin thrown over the mud. What else could they do? It was jolly effective anyway. There was no division for the male and female species, a thing pretty well frowned upon in those days. However, it was decided that we would grin and bare it and all promptly proceeded to dress for the show. We were almost ready when there was a tremendous outburst of cat-calls etcetera from the audience. Naturally, curiosity got the better and all peeped out to see what the rumpus was. How they wished they had been blessed with a cini camera to capture what must have been a unique incident of the war. There were four Rookies marching down the aisle. One with a bucket, one with a pail of water, one with a seat and the last, but by no means least ... with a toilet roll. The funniest sight the Party had really encountered

"RAF Beaulieu was another favourite place to visit and many good friends were made there. After a while, when they found we were in earnest, we had an almost permanent supply of petrol provided. How, well it was anybody's guess, one did not ask questions, but just take it and go."

RAF Beaulieu was perhaps the only Unit to be thoughtful enough at the end of the War to invite the Party to the first plush Hunt Ball; maybe it was there way of saying thank you. Strangely enough the Party received very little actual "thanks", they did not expect any. After all they were quite content to give of their services and get on with what they were doing. So, this invitation was really appreciated.

At the Party's 1,000 Show however, the most gratifying thing of all materialised. Southern Command presented the Party with a lovely "thank you" certificate. It was printed with the Southern Command emblem and highly cherished by Betty.

The Royal Victoria Army hospital at Netley was another favoured place to do a show. It was a lovely building in those days, but has now been razed to the ground. Some buildings have been erected behind where the old Hospital used to be, but fortunately the Officers Mess still remains.

Looking back with nostalgia about Netley Hospital, Betty wonders if the ghost – The Lady in Grey – still walks the corridors.

"The Unit, which stands out in memory from all others, is Holmsley Airfield," said Betty. *"Where we were actually giving a show on D-Day night. We were told that there might be disturbance in the audience as there was an operation due. We had no idea of the enormity of such a project, yet knew it was serious.*

"The Air Crews were coming and going the whole time and never ever before was any National Anthem taken away from us and sung so much with feeling by the whole audience. Even now, going on that disused airfield one is haunted by that singing as if it will never fade away. That memory can never be erased."

Betty's daughter Gloria was five years old when she started entertaining the Forces. Although she was that tender age, she was already attending dancing classes.

It was the Americans who started her giving shows to the Forces, and strangely enough she was very popular

Betty has been most welcomed, wined and dined at all Army, Naval and Air force Units. She has been on a submarine, helicopter, hovercraft, Gemini, rigid radar, "talk down" of a plane, Army Tanker and witnessed a Firing Display at Larkhill where she was the only woman present amongst High Ranking Officers from many countries.

Betty and Monica showing the Americans that they are the Best ... they certainly are.

Here we see Betty with our First Sea Lord Admiral Sir Jonathon Band GCB, DL, and ADC. Betty also had a nice picture taken with the Second Sea Lord Admiral Alan Massey KCB, CBE. Lovely to see you Betty in such fabulous company. Betty still visits the Carriers for lunch with the Captain.

DARK SECRETS

Here we see WAAF riggers at work on a Lysander

Charles Humphrey of Slough in Berkshire wrote to ask me if I had anything in my files about WAAFs - Women's Auxiliary Air Force - going on bombing raids during the Second World War. A very interesting question about the fairer sex.

In those days, unlike the women's lib brigade that we find around today, the WAAFs did not have to burn their bras.

At RAF Hibaldstow in Lincolnshire, Aircraftwoman Margaret Horton was sitting on the tail of Spitfire AB910 when the pilot suddenly took off, the pilot not noticing her until he was airborne. Fortunately, the Spitfire and its back-seat tail passenger landed safely after a complete circuit of the airfield.

ACW Horton should have been awarded something for her courage ... Surely she should have been.

In early 1943 the Germans claimed to have found the body of a WAAF in the wreckage of a Stirling bomber that had been shot down.

The Ministry denied it and, there is no official record of a WAAF being allowed on an operational bombing mission. But that does not mean it did not happen. It did happen; but this was obviously covered up.

Just stop to think how it would have looked informing the next of kin. The mother and father who thought their daughter was safe in an office or parachute room at some remote airfield, only to receive the dreaded telegram.

'The Queen Bee is sorry to inform you that your daughter is missing over Germany.'

On the night of 1st-2nd March 1943, a Stirling bomber was brought down near Mantgum in Holland. Eight bodies were recovered from the wreckage but RAF records show only seven airmen on board.

But, there was an eighth crew member; and it was a woman, a WAAF. In the local churchyard at Mantgum there are eight graves. And to support this, an RAF aircrew prisoner of war who could speak and read German, saw the story and photograph in a German newspaper.

In April 1945 a Liberator of No.86 Squadron based at Tain in the Western Highlands of Scotland, crashed in the sea off Helmsdale on the east coast of Scotland. RAF records show that motor launch 2587 raced to the position where the RAF Coastal Command bomber had crashed and picked up the only two survivors two WAAFs.

But now the mystery deepens. The records show that one WAAF soon died of her injuries, the other WAAF died before they could get her ashore.

The RAF records make no mention of the fact that a third WAAF was rescued by a fishing boat from the Helmsdale fleet.

She was taken to Dubrobin Castle, Golspie, which was then a military hospital. She recovered and she said that there had been four of them on board, herself, the WAAF who died, the pilot and flight engineer who were also killed in the crash.

That is very strange for RAF records show two died. So that is a mystery.

However, whatever the reason, you cannot deny that they were very brave and, for that reason, it should be brought out into the open.

Why should young British girls die in obscurity?

I, therefore, ask all female readers, especially former WAAFs to shed some light on this ... let us hear your 'dark secrets' of any unofficial wartime missions. Write to ANZIO now.

*Above we see WAAFs studying the layout of an airfield with the assistance of a model.
Left are two WAAFs loading ammunition belts. All WAAFs were a vital part of the war effort*

THE TELEPATHY INCIDENT

I do say on page 198 in Ghost Stations™ 5 that I will mention a very similar telepathy incident that happened to me; but first the story that I titled 'An Uncanny Occurrence' after I received an interesting letter from Robert Bell; and show the said letter from Robert so that you will understand. The actual letter as follows:

Dear Mr. Halpenny

As with your previous books, Ghost Stations V was an interesting and thought provoking read. However, this time, one particular extract took on greater relevance as it involved my late father. What I will relate cannot be regarded as a ghost story, but it does follow the theme of unexplained occurrences.

The extract I refer to is paragraph three and four on page 94 of the article "Strange Happenings at RAF Soerabaja", beginning with "The third case concerns a transport called the Lisbon Maru."

So let me explain, but first, let me explain the meaning of telepathy. It is the communication of impressions of any kind from one mind to another, independently of the recognised channels of sense. It connotes all communications between mind and mind, not only of persons who are at a considerable distance from each other, but also of those who happen to be in the same room, although in the latter case the communication was in the early days sometimes termed thought-transference.

In 1876 Professor Barrett drew attention to the fact that certain persons have the faculty of communicating and transferring ideas and impressions either spontaneously or intentionally. Sir Oliver Lodge assume the existence of a subconscious mind; where as Sir W. Crookes looked upon the phenomena of telepathy as result of brain waves or vibrations connecting mind with mind.

Briefly, that is telepathy ... so let us now continue with Robert Bell's letter.

Robert (Bertie) Bell - Robert's father served with the Royal Scots Unit and was one of the 371 British prisoners, along with 1,300 American captives who were aboard the Jap ship Lisbon Maru when it was torpedoed in October 1942 ... See newspaper cutting of the day ... Robert takes up the story: "Meanwhile, thousands of miles away in Edinburgh, my grandmother awoke suddenly and turning to her husband said: ... **'Our son's in danger, he's in water.'**

"My father explained that after the war ... his mother recounted this story to him and when they worked out the dates … **it transpired that her sudden awakening coincided with him swimming for his life."**

POWs Locked in as Ship Sank

JAPS locked 371 British prisoners in the hold of a torpedoed ship and in another case packed 1,300 American captives into the coal bunkers of a ferry.

The survivors of these grim experiences told their stories yesterday.

The British soldiers, captured when Hong Kong fell, were aboard the 7,000-ton Jap ship Lisbon Maru when it was torpedoed in October, 1942.

The Japs locked the soldiers in the holds and went about rescuing 2,000 of their own men who were aboard.

Not a single Jap was lost, but 870 British were drowned.

"The Japs wouldn't let us get out of the holds. We lay in them all that day after the torpedoing," survivors said in Osaka yesterday after being liberated.

"The Japs battened down the hatches and pulled a tarpaulin over us. Water started seeping in. We pumped from seven o'clock that night until nine the next morning. The only water we had to drink was moisture that condensed on the bulkheads.

"At nine on the second night there was a sudden lurch. We broke the hatches open and found that the afterpart of the ship was afloat. We jumped overboard, but were not picked up by the Japs until the next afternoon."

Salt water was all there was to drink for the 1,300 American prisoners loaded into the coal bunkers of a Jap ferry after being taken from the prison camp at Manila.

They were told they would be transferred in a few hours. Thirty-eight days later survivors mad with thirst and near suffocation, dragged themselves up from the holds.

"It was worse than the march from Bataan," said the Americans. "Men starved to death and were beaten to death then. In the ship they suffocated and died from the heat."

As stated at the start let me now briefly explain the telepathy incident that involved me, and to do so will quote from my book: TOP SECRET RAF BARNHAM & I, for I have explained this fully on pages 23 and 24. Briefly then, I was on the way to the operating theatre one Sunday night and was just passing Sister's office at five minutes to midnight, when Sister's telephone suddenly started ringing. Sister went quickly to answer the telephone and I clearly heard her say: "He's all right. He is in good hands. I will tell him you telephoned." …

Sister came out of her office looking very serious; and she stood looking at me for a few moments, then seeing her eyes move to mine as if to speak, I quickly said: **"That was my mother, wasn't it?"** Sister, looking directly at me, lips tight and clearly holding back a tear, nodded that it was.

A WARTIME INCIDENT

One, if not the strangest incident of the Second World War, happened at RAF West Malling in Kent on the night of 16th April 1943. A single-engined aircraft was heard to approach the airfield; and after circling low over the airfield twice, it landed. Assuming that it was a Defiant aircraft, one of the ground crew climbed on to the wing to help the pilot out. As he did so he spotted the German markings on the fuselage and on seeing same he hastily jumped off, meeting as he did so an officer coming from the Control Tower to arrest the pilot.

By this time the fire-tender and crash crew also drove out; and at the same time another aircraft came in to land, this also being a German aircraft. The first pilot gave himself up; but the second pilot must have had second thoughts, or realized his mistake and tried to take off. As he did so some shots were fired from the fire tender and they obviously hit the oxygen bottles in the pilot's cockpit for the aircraft exploded.

A third German aircraft landed in the orchard after he over-shot the runway and a fourth German aircraft crashed into trees at Staplehurst.

Apparently, about fifteen German Focke-Wulf 190 fighters had been sent over England on intruder operations and had mistaken West Malling airfield for occupied Europe. The ground crews were told that the reason the German pilots had landed was that they were lost and were enticed down, in German, by the officer in charge of the Control Tower.

Well, you certainly must agree that it was a very strange incident.

DISHONOURED – DISOWNED

Joe Louis and Billy Conn entertain personnel on the Base at Barkston Heath in Lincolnshire.

Because so many aircrews met violent deaths and have no known graves, this gave rise to a legend that the old abandoned airfields are haunted. Official Mythology has fuelled this belief ... as explained in the File: Official Mythology.

This explains fully, about those who fought and gave their all, having been told it was for a better world, only to have their families and loved ones left in the lurch by the authorities.

And things have not changed today... One little Hitler now replaced with a host of little Hitler's and little Tin Gods.

In 1994 an RAF Chinook crashed in the Mull of Kintyre, killing the crew of four and all its passengers ... ten RUC Special Branch detectives, nine Army Officers and five men and a woman from MI5.

In June 1995, it was made known that the Ministry of Defence might use a legal device to limit compensation payments. The MoD was taking the unprecedented step of limiting liability to just over £100,000 per victim by describing the RAF as an air transport undertaking.

Doctor Susan Phoenix, whose husband Ian was one of those killed in the crash, said:

"The government has dishonoured our men."

No wonder there is so many restless Spirits and with such shabby betrayal, it is easy to understand why. And to add insult to injury, the report into the Chinook crash is ... from my own military experience... bound to find that it was pilot error.

With the pilot killed and not able to defend himself, it is odds on chance that he will get the blame. He did. The report (?) said that the crash was due to pilot error.

However, to make it look good, some will get medals. In the war the widows got a printed letter from the king ... that certainly helped to feed the family.

Joe Louis, world heavyweight boxing champion, had the Armed Forces in strength at his funeral, for he was known and respected the world over. This great American boxer, known as the "Brown Bomber" held the heavyweight championship of the world from 1937 to 1949 and defended his title 25 times.

Among those who tried without success to take the title from him were the Welshman Tommy Farr, the German Max Schmeling, Tony Galento, Bob Pastor, Billy Conn, Tami Mauriello and Jersey Joe Walcott.

From 1942 to 1945 Joe Louis served in the United States Army and during this period, gave exhibitions of boxing at army, navy and air force camps.

So it was a different story with Joe Louis, for he was famous.

Or was it …?

Yes, there was a huge turnout for his funeral, the American flag was draped over his coffin, Armed Forces in full ceremonial strength and the world press and television, as one would rightly expect for a hero and one who had served his country well.

America was proud to show the world that they do not forget a hero.

But it was all false. What they did not say was that for the last 15 years of his life he had lived in poverty.

The German boxer Max Schmeling could not attend the funeral but sent an envelope with some money in it for his wife and, on seeing the money, Mrs Louis said:

"Max Schmeling ... our only true friend."

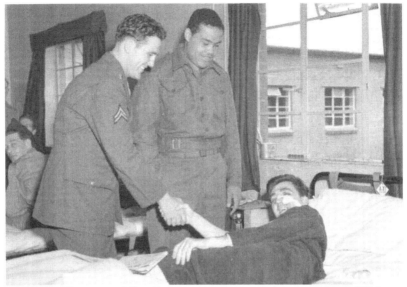

Billy Conn and Joe Louis visit men of the American IXth
AFTCC in hospital at Barkston Lincolnshire.

Take the case of Horatio Nelson (1758 - 1805), the most famous naval commander of the greatest maritime power in history. What does the nation owe him?

A king's ransom…?

His flagship, HMS Victory, brought the news home and England learned with pride ... is pride not a dirty word? ... No, with pride of her greatest naval victory since the defeat of the Armada.

Nelson was mortally wounded in the hour of victory and on his death, Lady Nelson was given a pension of £2,000 a year and his brother, the Reverend William Nelson, was created Earl Nelson of Trafalgar with a pension of £5,000 a year.

This pension continued to be paid for over 100 years; until in 1946 an Act of Parliament was passed ending the payment on the deaths of the 4th Earl (who died in 1947) and his brother.

Up to 1946 about £70,000 had been paid to the holders of the title of Earl Nelson. The 5th Earl then decided that Trafalgar House near Salisbury, which was given to the Nelson family, would be sold, though the relics of Horatio Nelson were to be presented to the National Maritime Museum at Greenwich.

But what of Lady Hamilton…?

Though several times during his dying moments, Nelson whispered:

"Look after poor Lady Hamilton."

Nelson's dying wish was not carried out. Nothing was done for her by the State or Nelson's so-called friends; and sadly, Lady Hamilton, a very, very beautiful woman who, was Nelson's mistress, died in poverty in Calais, France in 1815.

Those out to discredit Lady Hamilton have it that she died in 1817, in France. You have the true date and story from me.

That is the state … dishonoured … disowned. The state quickly forgot Nelson's dying wish and his signal:

His wish: to look after Lady Hamilton... his signal: England expects that every man will do his duty. We are told about the bad old days, how bad things were; but were they? Arrian, a Roman historian in the second century AD, wrote:

'The day after the battle of Issus in 333BC, Alexandra The Great, ordered that all those killed were to be buried with their weapons. Their parents and children back home in Macedonia were granted immunity from local taxes.'

In the so-called civilised world of the 21st Century, the reward for war pensioners and war widows is to make them suffer on a paltry pension. They are too proud to beg.

In today's 21st century lawless Britain under new Labour, if you are a pensioner, Family householder or a lone woman, you are at real risk of a vicious assault and your assailants will not be caught. If immigrants, the police will not arrest for fear of riots.

This despair and failure to look after those who fought, and their families, could be the culminating fact why there are so many restless Spirits that now haunt this once green and pleasant land.

Dishonoured ... Disowned.

Those little Hitler's and little Tin Gods should remember the dying words of Lieutenant - Colonel John Alexander McCrae: "Tell them this ... if ye break faith with us who die ... we shall not sleep."

THE MAN WHO NEVER WAS

Two weeks after his 21st birthday David Petrie joined the Royal Air Force VR in July 1942. After a period in the Middle East, he returned to the United Kingdom, and after a week's disembarkation leave, he was posted to RAF Manston in Kent.

RAF Manston was one of three Bomber Command Emergency Landing Grounds - the other two being Woodbridge in Suffolk and Carnaby in Yorkshire. All three were coastal airfields specially designed to handle crippled bombers in any kind of situation. With the aid of FIDO, landings could be made in all weather conditions. Manston was also fully equipped with emergency services.

Sergeant David Petrie arrived at RAF Manston in April 1944 and he was put in charge of a crash crew section. It was a job that needed a lot of stomach and within days he was cutting out dead and wounded aircrew from shot-up bombers.

It was just after D-Day and Sergeant Petrie was again on duty. One morning just after 11 a.m. Manston received information that there was a crippled bomber limping home across the channel and trying to make it to the emergency airfield. The message was conveyed to the crash crew and upon receipt of it Sergeant Petrie and his crew raced down the special long runway to a point nearest to an estimated crash landing.

After a short wait a Lancaster bomber crash-landed with its port undercarriage damaged, consequently it skidded across the runway and caught in some wire netting with its starboard wing high in the air. The port inner was feathered when it crashed and smoke was coming from the starboard outer engine.

The crippled bomber still had its full crew on board and as the aircraft screeched to a stop, the crew made a hurried exit and in so doing the pilot left the engine running. The crash crew were there by the time the bomber halted and quickly sizing up the situation; Sergeant Petrie decided to eliminate any risk of fire and boarded the aircraft to switch the engine off. On entering the aircraft he met a civilian wearing a brown pin-stripe suit and told him that he had better get out quick because of the risk of fire. Sergeant Petrie gave him no more thought as he was having difficulty in trying to locate the switch.

"The next thing that I knew was that a man leaned across and switched the engine off," said Sergeant Petrie. After making sure that everything was safe Sergeant Petrie made his way out of the aircraft as quickly as possible and, as he turned to walk away, saw an elderly RAF Sergeant standing near the door of the aircraft. On seeing the Sergeant, Sergeant Petrie asked him if he could tell him where the civilian in the brown pin-stripe suit had gone, as he would like to thank him for perhaps saving his life.

"You must be seeing things," replied the Sergeant. "There are no civilians allowed on this airfield." Sergeant Petrie did not believe the Sergeant for he had seen him, spoken to him and, as he was the only person in the aircraft with him, he had to be the person who switched off the engine.

Sergeant Petrie would not take no for an answer and throughout the day he persistently asked the other Sergeant about the civilian. He was repeatedly told:

"Forget it son - there was no one there other than the crew, only you came out of the Lancaster."

After eight months at RAF Manston, Sergeant Petrie was posted to No.2 Armoured Car Company, Aden, in January 1945 and he remained in Aden until October 1946, from where he was demobbed.

Four decades later ex-Sergeant Petrie is still adamant about the figure he saw in the crippled Lancaster bomber. Someone switched off the engine and he knows that it could only have been the civilian in the brown pin-stripe suit. Had he seen his Guardian Angel?

I think that was certainly the case; and deep down, I am positive that Sergeant Petrie knows that to be so.

THE HAUNTED BOMBER

The Royal Air Force Museum at Cosford in Shropshire has its own resident ghost - called Fred. The ghost was first seen after the arrival of a Lincoln bomber, No. RF398 in 1977.

The early post-war bomber was in need of repairs and one in charge was ex-RAF engineer John Small who had serviced Lincolns in the Middle and Far East.

"The first time I saw the phantom airman I was speechless," said John. "He was sitting on a toolbox inside the Lincoln. Then he vanished."

Many of the volunteers working on the Lincoln have seen the phantom airman in blue battledress jacket and a white polo-neck sweater.

Many people have heard footsteps coming along the fuselage only to turn and see no one there.

The ghost airman has been seen; not only in the Lincoln bomber, but also in the hangar, by a great many people. Also, since the appearance of the phantom airman there has been some strange goings on.

- Strange whistling of an unidentifiable tunc has been heard many times in the museum.

- Another time an engineer working on the Lincoln bomber fell backwards to the floor without hurting himself.

- And, during a very cold spell the aircraft interior was warm enough to work in without a jacket.

"It is all very eerie," said John Small, "so very puzzling, but everything that happens appears to be for the Lincoln bomber. The job of rewiring through the wings should have taken weeks but it was done in 48 hours."

One Sunday afternoon in September 1980, Mrs Greaves of Cannock, Staffordshire was visiting the Museum at Cosford.

"It was about 4 p.m.," she said. "I looked up to the cockpit of the Lincoln bomber and saw a figure of a fair-haired man in a white polo neck sweater and wearing a forage cap. I felt very puzzled on seeing the figure and it bothered me for a day or two, because he was not in regulation uniform."

Mrs Greaves added: "He appeared to be an officer to me, and I just felt he should not have been there in the cockpit."

There are one or two theories about the phantom airman. "One is that it could be a Spitfire pilot who was killed when his aircraft crashed," said Mr Small.

"It was refurbished and put in the hangar. But it has gone, and the phantom airman is still here."

Another theory is that it is the ghost of an engineer who killed himself when the bomber he was responsible for crashed in the late 1940s killing all the crew. Some parts of the crashed bomber found their way into the hangar.

There have been other theories about the phantom airman being an engineer, for during the war, over 70,000 engine and airframe mechanics and armourers passed through Cosford.

The Station opened in 1938 and throughout the war years RAF Cosford housed No.9 Maintenance Unit in No. 41 Group and they handled many kinds of aircraft, but the main ones were Spitfires and Wellingtons.

Also, the RAF Military Hospital was established at Cosford during the war. So, there are many theories for the phantom airman.

One thing is certain - he is at home in the old Lincoln bomber.

THE HAUNTED ROAD

A phantom roadside figure has been sighted not far from High Wycombe in Buckinghamshire.

High Wycombe was the home of RAF Bomber Command during the Second World War, the area was chosen because of - its remoteness.

It was at High Wycombe that Air Marshal Sir Arthur T. Harris took over as Commander-in-Chief of Bomber Command on 3 February 1942.

From High Wycombe Harris hatched his plots to destroy the industrial might of Germany. And in the process kill thousands of innocent civilians, with his needless bombing of non-strategic targets.

By the end of the Second World War, Bomber Command had dropped over two million high explosive bombs and 83 million incendiaries, equal to one bomb dropped every two seconds throughout the days and nights of the war.

The cost in terms of life was high; some 47,000 aircrew were killed, many just blasted out of the skies and it was Harris at High Wycombe who gave the orders.

One night in January 1971, Steve Bond and his wife were driving home to their house in High Wycombe, along the main A404 road from Amersham, at around 15 minutes past midnight.

Along this section of the road there are wide grass verges on both side and, the long sweeping curves and good straight stretches, make it a fast road.

The night was cold and clear with not much traffic about, as Steve Bond explains:

"There was not much traffic about so I was able to drive on full-beam headlights.

"As we negotiated one of the curves, I could see for several hundred yards ahead that the road was empty in an instant a figure appeared standing in the side of the road half facing towards us.

"The appearance was so sudden that I had to swerve to avoid it, there was absolutely no cover from behind which the figure could have appeared.

"In the couple of seconds during which it was in full view of my headlights, it could be seen to be a figure of a stocky man in what I would describe as a sports jacket; his head was completely wrapped in bandages, but he had no face at all, just a sort of greyness.

"There was a car some short distance behind me and I checked my mirror to see if he too pulled out. He did not.

"And despite being on a curve, the figure was not as I would have expected, silhouetted.

"Neither of us spoke for some time, until I asked my wife if she had seen anything; we subsequently described the same thing exactly; but were too nervous to go back for another look."

So what had Steven Bond and his wife seen, that January morning?

Was it one of Harris's faceless aircrew come back to haunt the area around High Wycombe?

So many brave aircrew needlessly died during the Second World War and this is made clear in other Stories in the **Ghost Stations Series**; very much so in my book **Ghost Stations™ Germany**.

Over the years there have been many phantom sightings on that stretch of road near High Wycombe.

The incident with Steven Bond and his wife took place about halfway between Amersham and High Wycombe just before the B474 turning to Beaconsfield.

Another eerie incident that happened on that stretch of haunted road was indeed very chilling.

The brother-in-law of Steve Bond was following a car along the A404 road, along that same piece of road, when he noticed that the car in front appeared to have an injured person slumped in the back.

The driver frequently looked over his shoulder anxiously to check his passenger.

They were heading towards High Wycombe and concerned at what he had seen, he asked at the hospital in High Wycombe about the patient recently admitted, only to be told ... no one had been admitted.

THE GHOST CREWS RETURN

First used during the First World War when it was called Harpswell after the small hamlet that lay at the southern end of the airfield.

After the First World War the site was reclaimed for agricultural use and all traces of the airfield were soon eradicated ... but not the ghosts.

In the early 1930's the site was selected to serve the expanding Royal Air Force and work began on building an airfield. It was one of the earliest of the Expansion Bomber bases.

The new bomber airfield, known as Hemswell after the village immediately to its west, opened in January 1937 in Number 5 Group, Bomber Command.

During the war years the main flying units were 61 and 144 Squadrons at the start of the war; then arrived two Polish squadrons, No.300 and No.301.

Another Polish Squadron, No.305, joined them. In the summer of 1943 the Polish Squadrons moved to Ingham in Lincolnshire and Hemswell closed for several months while the runways were laid.

The airfield re-opened in January 1944 when No.1 Group Lancaster Finishing School (LFS) arrived and remained non-operational until November 1944 when No.1 LFS moved out to be replaced by two Lancaster Squadrons.

After the war Hemswell remained a bomber airfield for many years; then, in the Sixties it was used for training until vacated by the Royal Air Force in 1967.

Early one morning in 1972 a delivery driver was nearing the entrance to RAF Hemswell on the A631 when he suddenly had to brake sharp when two airmen in flying clothes crossed in front of him.

The driver screeched to a stop and his anger turned to amazement, then fear, when the two airmen turned to look at him and then vanished.

Jim and Molly Thompson also had a similar encounter with the ghost airmen.

They had parked at the side of the A631, just past the entrance for RAF Hemswell, when Jim saw two airmen standing at the roadside, as if waiting to cross the road.

"I rushed towards them in order to ask them who to see to get onto the airfield and as I shouted they both turned, looked at me, then started to cross the road to what I later found out was the Officers' Mess; but they never made it across the road for after a few paces they just disappeared," said Jim Thompson.

Many people have reported seeing airmen on or near the entrance to RAF Hemswell on the A631 ... mostly at dawn and at dusk. Are they the lost crews returning?

Over the past fifteen years the sightings have got more numerous along the stretch of A631 near the entrance to RAF Hemswell.

A postman said he passed two RAF Officers who were talking in a foreign language and on turning to see where they were going found that they had vanished.

Other ghostly happenings on the old airfield have also been reported; many recorded in Ghost Stations™, one of the best being Derek Harrison's encounter ... The Missouri Waltz; that Derek told exclusively to me for the Ghost Stations™ Series.

As we enter the 21st century a vast number of wartime buildings still remain, although no runway survives, only parts of the perimeter track.

Sadly, this once proud and historic bomber station has gone down the road of destruction like so many wartime airfields and it has been turned into yet another industrial estate.

Only the former Officers' Mess to the south of the A631 tried to retain some sort of decorum befitting its former role by becoming the Hemswell Cliff Hotel. Sadly, it went out of business.

It is a fact that the Officers' Mess is on the south side of the A631 and the ghost airmen could be returning to the Mess ... for many it could have been their last place on earth.

As for the two phantom Officers speaking a foreign language, they could have been Polish Airmen, which would explain that; for a great many Polish aircrews were missing from RAF Hemswell.

Had they witnessed the ghost crews returning?

BY A STRANGE COINCIDENCE

In 1952 Major Robert Jones was in the Golden Hind public house at Manadon; Plymouth and this is his story, that I have titled: By A Strange Coincidence, told in his own words:

"I was in the Golden Hind pub by myself, when a gentleman walked in, and being the only two there besides Ron, the barman, we passed the time of day.

"One thing led to another, and eventually the conversation turned to the war and the Far East. It turned out that he was the area manager for Hoover, a gentleman by the name of Mister Cann, and had been a Major in a British Commando Unit.

"He told me of an incident in Burma by a strange coincidence, in which I had later become involved, when he had come across a very large gravel quarry with trees growing in the centre.

"Stripped and tied to the trees were three Australian nurses, and surrounded by several Japanese, obviously with evil intent.

"Major Cann had to decide how they should be rescued and deployed his men accordingly; but on the first shot being fired the women were slit from bottom to top with knives. Horrible and unnecessary deaths but typical of what we met all too often."

Captain (later Major) Robert Jones was with a War Graves Unit serving with War Crimes Investigation ... see THE GHOSTS OF THE SOUTH CHINA SEAS and STRANGE HAPPENINGS AT RAF SOERABAJA in Ghost Stations™.

"In my job we saw the evidence and even at second hand it wasn't pleasant," said Major Jones.

The above true story highlights how by a strange coincidence they should meet like that. Major Cann leading the Commando Force when the Japanese carried out the evil deed; and Major Jones leading the War Crimes Investigation team that investigated the brutal murders.

THE VANISHING 3000

In an effort to remove the Nationalist government of Chiang Kaishek, the Japanese occupied large areas of eastern China in 1937 and 1938.

Nanking fell in 1937.

Nanking is situated on the southeast bank of the Yangtze, some 160 miles from Shanghai. Just to the south of the city, the Chinese Commander decided to make a stand and called for 3000 reinforcements.

When the troops arrived they were deployed close to the main bridge across the Yangtze River. The soldiers dug in with their heavy guns and the Commander returned to his headquarters that was a mile or so behind the lines.

Just after dawn the Commander was awoken with the news that they could not contact the 3000 strong force. Upon investigation the complete army of men had vanished … all 3000 of them. The guns were still in position but the men who manned them had vanished.

The actual soldiers guarding the bridge were still at their posts and they testified that no one had crossed the bridge, nor had they heard anything suspicious.

It was incredible for 3000 men could not just vanish into thin air, yet they had done so. None of the guards on the bridge had heard or seen anything. It was impossible for all 3000 men to desert and even if they had done so, surely someone would have heard them.

But the Japanese gave them no time to solve the baffling mystery, for Nanking fell the following day. In the sack of the city that followed, the Japanese slaughtered more than 40,000 civilians.

This appalling atrocity became known as the 'Rape of Nanking'. Puppet governments ruled the city until Japan's defeat in 1945 by the Allies, which ended their occupation of China.

The 'Rape of Nanking' overshadowed the vanishing 3000 and they are today regarded as casualties of war. Just another mystery of the Second World War ... an unexplained mystery of the vanishing 3000.

STRANGE HAPPENINGS AT RAF SOERABAJA

On another occasion in 1946, Captain Jones was sent to investigate the crash of an RAF bomber at RAF Soerabaja. The bomber, a Vultee Vengeance, had mysteriously crashed on the airfield and the crew suspected of being murdered. It is interesting to note that No 84 Squadron was using its Vengeance bombers to bomb the Japanese just south of Homalin, in Burma, when suddenly; they were taken off operations with the old Vultee Vegeance bomber and re-equipped with de Havilland Mosquitoes. But they had a sinister problem with the Mosquitoes and, for some unknown reason; they were withdrawn and, were never used against the Japanese. "A great pity," said Corporal Smith of the RAF Ground Staff. "The old Mossie would have blasted the yellow bastards off the face of the earth."

At this period, Captain Jones was stationed at Sonoabaja in Eastern Java; while most of his unit remained at Singapore. For that reason he had to use Japanese prisoners-of-war as labour, and it was they who made the twelve coffins. Captain Jones explains:

"The boxes were about six feet by two feet by eighteen inches, simple and plain. We had completed our gruesome task, putting what remains could be found into the plain coffins and, I was just taking a rest.

"Suddenly one of the coffins started 'walking' away on to one side then its front, then the other side, then its back ... and so on. We all froze in utter amazement. Nobody was nearer than six to eight feet at the time, mostly sitting down resting. After the initial shock of seeing the coffin 'walking' away, the Japs fled and I had to bring them back by firing over their heads.

Drawing by Captain Jones to show movement of 'walking coffin'.

"The reason? Your guess is as good as mine. It could not have been the sun warping the wood for the coffin did not falter in its movement and only came to a halt after hitting a case some thirty feet away."

So what made the coffin walk in the noonday sun at RAF Soerabaja? Were those murdered by the despicable Japanese trying to haunt them? It is a fact that the Japanese are great believers in the vengeance of their ancestors. And, the Japanese have a lot to answer for. Let us look at the facts and hear what the Right Honourable Anthony Eden, Secretary of State for Foreign Affairs had to say in 1944.

Speaking in the House of Commons on 28th January 1944, on the treatment of allied prisoners in the hands of the Japanese. Mr Anthony Eden said: "I fear I have grave news to give the House. Members will be aware that a large number of postcards and letters have recently been received in this country from prisoners in the Far East; and that these almost uniformly suggest that the writers are being treated well and are in good health. There is no doubt from what we know about particular areas that some of these communications, at any rate, are in terms dictated by the Japanese authorities. I regret to have to tell the House that information which has been reaching his Majesty's Government no longer leaves room for any doubt that the true state of affairs is a very different one so far as the great majority of prisoners in Japanese hands is concerned.

"The House is already aware that a very high proportion, perhaps 80 to 90 per cent, of the prisoners and civilian internees in Japanese hands are located in the southern area, comprising the Philippine Islands, the Netherlands, East Indies, Borneo, Malaya, Burma, Siam, and Indo-China, and that the Japanese Government have hitherto withheld permission for any neutral inspection of any of the camps in question. We have not even been allowed to know the numbers of prisoners detained in the various areas, nor have the names of a large number of those who must have been taken prisoner by the Japanese yet been communicated to us.

"For some time past information has been reaching his Majesty's Government regarding the conditions under which prisoners are detained and worked in some of these areas, and as it was of so grave a character as to be likely to cause distress to relatives of prisoners and civilian internees in Japanese hands his Majesty's Government felt bound to satisfy themselves that it was authentic before making it public. We are now so satisfied and it becomes my painful duty to tell the House that in Siam there are many thousands of prisoners from the British Commonwealth, including India, who are being compelled by the Japanese military to live in tropical jungle conditions without adequate shelter, clothing, food, or medical attention; and these men are forced to work on building a railway and making roads. Our information is that their health is rapidly deteriorating, that a high percentage are seriously ill, and that there have been some thousands of deaths. Here may I add that the number of such deaths reported by the Japanese to us is just over 100. The railway and roads concerned lead into Burma, and the conditions I have described apply throughout there whole length.

"One eye-witness reports of a camp in Siam that 'I saw many prisoners clearly; they were skin and bone, unshaven and with long matted hair; they were half-naked.' The same witness reported that they wore no hats or shoes; and this, may I remind the House, in a tropical climate, where the neighbouring country is virtually uninhabited, so that there are practically no local resources which could provide medical or other material relief.

"Of one other part of this huge southern area we have some information. From Java comes evidence which leaves no doubt that many of our prisoners are confined in camps with no adequate protection from malarial infection and lacking in proper provision for sanitation; except in so far as prisoners may sometimes obtain food from local sources, the food and clothing provided is insufficient to maintain them in health. Reports from the northern area have referred to the emaciated state of prisoners arriving from Java. I have so far no information to give the House regarding conditions in other parts of the Southern area.

"Before I leave the Southern area, there is one exception I can make to what I have said. There are civilians interned in our old military camp at Changi and in the neighbourhood of Bangkok and Saigon, and our information suggests that conditions of those particular camps are at least tolerable.

"The refusal of the Japanese Government to permit neutral inspections of camps in the southern area is difficult to understand, in view of the fact that they have allowed visits by neutral inspectors, though on a scale which we cannot regard as adequate, to camps in the northern area, which comprises Hong Kong, Formosa, Shanghai, Korea, and Japan itself. His Majesty's Government are reasonably satisfied that conditions generally in this area are tolerable, though as the Secretary of State for War has said on more than one occasion, the scale on which food is provided is not adequate over long periods to maintain the health of prisoners. I should add, however, that conditions in Hong Kong appear to be growing worse.

"If that were the whole of the story it would be bad indeed; but there is unhappily worse to come. We have a growing list of cases of brutal outrage on individuals or groups of individuals. I could not burden the House with the full tale of these. But in order to give an idea of their nature I must, I fear, quote a few typical examples. First, two cases affecting civilians.

"The first is that of an officer in the Shanghai Municipal Police Force. Along with some 200 other allied nationals he was interned by the Japanese in the detention camp for so-called political suspects at Haiphong Road in Shanghai. He incurred the displeasure of the Japanese gendarmerie and was taken away to their office in another part of the town.

"When he emerged from the building he was practically out of his mind; his arms and feet were infected where ropes had left - deep scars; and he had lost 40 lb of weight. He died within a day or two of his release.

"The second case comes from the Philippine Islands. Here, on 11th February 1942, three British subjects escaped from the Japanese civilian internment camp at Santo Tomas, Manila. They were recaptured and flogged by the camp guard. Two days later, on 14th February, they were sentenced to death by a military court, despite the fact that international law prescribes the imposition of only disciplinary punishment for attempts to escape. The firing party used automatic pistols, and the three men were not killed outright.

"I now turn to cases affecting soldiers. A number of Indian soldiers captured in Burma, having had their hands tied behind their backs, were made to sit in groups by the side of the road. They were then systematically bayoneted from behind in turn, each man receiving apparently three bayonet thrusts. By some miracle, one man who collapsed subsequently recovered and escaped to our lines. That's how we know.

"The other case concerns an officer of a well-known regiment of the line, who was captured in Burma. After being clubbed across the face with a sword he was tied to a stake and a rope was passed round his neck so that only by raising his body could he just get enough air to keep him alive. He was then subjected to further torture. Fortunately an allied attack developed, the Japanese fled. and the officer was rescued by a British tank.

"The third case concerns a transport called the Lisbon Maru which was being used to convey over 1,800 British prisoners of war from Hong Kong. Conditions on board were almost indescribable. The prisoners were seriously overcrowded. Many of them were undernourished and many had contracted diphtheria, dysentery, and other diseases. There was no medical provision; and the sanitary arrangements were virtually non-existent. Two of the prisoners in one hold died where they lay, and no attempt was made to remove their bodies.

"On the morning of 1st October, 1942, the vessel was torpedoed by a United Nations submarine. The Japanese officers, soldiers, and crew kept the prisoners under hatches and abandoned ship forthwith although she did not sink until 24 hours later. There were insufficient lifebelts and other safety appliances on board. Some of the prisoners managed to break out and swim to land. They were fired on when in the water. In all, at least 800 prisoners lost their lives.

"I have said sufficient to show the barbarous nature of our Japanese enemy. He has violated not only the principles of international law but all canons of decent and civilized conduct. His Majesty's Government has repeatedly made the strongest possible representations to the Japanese Government through the Swiss Government. Such replies as have been received have been evasive, cynical, or otherwise unsatisfactory. We had the right to expect that, once aware of the facts, the Japanese Government would remedy this state of affairs. The Japanese know well what are the obligations of a civilized Power to safeguard the life and health of prisoners who have fallen into their hands. This was shown by their treatment of prisoners in the Russo-Japanese war and the war of 1914-1918. Let the Japanese Government reflect that in time to come the record of their military authorities in this war will not be forgotten.

"It is with the deepest regret that I have been obliged to make such a statement to the House. But after consultation with their allies who are equally victims of this unspeakable savagery, his Majesty's Government have felt it to be their duty to make public the facts."

Those are the facts. That is the reason why the coffin walked. It was in shame for Jap atrocities of war are glossed over. In 1945, a defeated Japan that had inflicted horrendous atrocities on all prisoners of war and, their Asian neighbours expected the worse from the conquering heroes. By this period Eden was dancing to the American tune. What about war crimes? Instead the Americans made them what they are today. But what about them being tried for war crimes? The Germans were and, still are, as we have seen recently in Israel.

That is why the coffin 'walked' at RAF Soerabaja.

Captain Jones and Two Australians on one of the South Sea Islands on route to RAF Soerabaja

THE HEADLESS GHOSTS

Canon Finnay, during the Ghost Watch-1987 radio programme told in this volume of **Ghost Stations™** said: "An actual figure of a man wandering round the tower with his head under his arm is a very rare beast indeed … and to be frank I have never come across anything of that kind."

But many people have reported seeing headless ghosts. Are they all wrong? Even some American Servicemen have claimed to have seen a headless ghost.; who they call Lakenheath Charlie.

Over the years there have been many tales of Lakenheath Charlie emerging from the American Air Force Base at RAF Lakenheath in Suffolk. Nearly all the hauntings are in the area around the notorious Tab-Vee 46 shelter, or mini-hangar as it is sometimes called; whatever it is called, it is a very haunted hangar and area all around the hangar.

"You get such a weird feeling when you get near Tab-Vee 46," said, one security policeman. Another policeman on foot-patrol re-ported seeing a misty figure, "Could not make out the figure of a man," he said. "Just a misty figure … that was only body and legs. It was really weird … and frightening.

"My sergeant saw it a few nights later and he was as scared as anyone. When he saw the ghost he was in Red Section and just behind the Tab-Vee 46 shelter."

One night ... the lights were reported flashing on and off in Tab-Vee 46 and the airfield security police quickly rushed to the shelter.

"When we got there I thought I heard gunshots from inside the shelter, said a Military Police Sergeant, "I then got the strange feeling that somebody was behind me ... I turned sharply to see this strange ghostly figure; who disappeared when it got to within a few feet of me. I just cannot explain it."

Many people think that Lakenheath Charlie is the ghost of an RAF pilot who crashed near the Tab-Vee 46 shelter during the last war. In the crash the pilot was decapitated and people say it is the ghost of the pilot looking for his head.

True or false? One thing is certain, and that is, there have been many unexplained happenings in and around Tab-Vee 46. Tools have just disappeared, and items have been moved around, as if by unseen hands; and that is all so very strange, as those who work in the haunted ... eerie Tab-Vee 46.

"It was almost too much for me," said one maintenance man. "Let me give you one eerie incident. On one occasion a mechanic was lying on the floor whilst working on the underside of an aircraft inside Tab-Vee 46. His companion was handing him tools from time to time as needed. The man helping was suddenly called away and when he returned and apologized to the other mechanic for being away longer than expected, the other man was taken-aback; for he had not known that he had gone for someone had continued to pass the tools."

Many ghostly stories have filtered out from RAF Lakenheath ... all very interesting, for I often paid visits to Lakenheath to compare security during my Service days with the Royal Air Force Military Police Special Duties Force. It was tight then for security. Now it seems that if there is any breach of security or unexplained happening ... they chalk up another for Lakenheath Charlie.

From one headless ghost to another. This one has been seen ... very clearly ... to become known as the Headless Ghost of Snowdonia. But, let us go back and start at the beginning.

Over the years, Snowdon in North Wales, with its five distinct peaks, has claimed many victims, many of these being through aircraft that came to grief in the mountains. During the war years there were many. One such incident occurred around 0300 hours on the 14th April 1941, when a German aircraft crashed into the mountain side of Snowdonia.

A few hours earlier the twin-engined Heinkel bomber, from the 1st Staffel of KG28, had taken off from its base at St. Malo in France, to attack the shipyards at Barrow-in-Furness. But the German bomber was destined not to return.

Near the target area the Heinkel was hit by Ack-Ack fire. Then it was engaged by a night-fighter, and during a hit and run chase, the Heinkel bomber received direct hits, which knocked out the radio-set, and compass. The German pilot had survived the Ack-Ack guns and the night-fighter attack; but was now without radio and compass and, still over England.

He set course for home using the night sky and any other landmarks available; but the pilot was miles off course and he was heading for disaster. At approximately 0300 hours the German bomber hit the plateau above Aber Falls in Wales. Miraculously, all the crew but for the Flight Engineer, survived the crash. In the impact the Flight Engineer was decapitated.

This crash happened in the early days of the war, when there were numerous crashes ... many from Royal Air Force bombers returning shot-up from missions and many during training flights. Many of the aircraft that crashed in mountains and other open spaces were never recovered. Many were never found; not even to this day. They were listed as missing and are still missing.

A few years ago a party of aviation enthusiasts were climbing on section above Aber Falls, when they came upon the wreckage of the Heinkel bomber. Being aviation enthusiasts they realized the importance of their find and, knew it was a World War Two German aircraft. They immediately split up in order to examine the widely dispersed pieces of the wreckage.

Whilst the others set about a much wider search, one member of the party was left to examine the Jumo engines from the crashed bomber. He was very excited and became too engrossed in his find to note a ghostly figure; then suddenly he became aware of a uniformed figure, sitting on a nearby rock … he looked across at the ghostly figure; and his blood ran cold when he saw, what looked like a plastic bag or small sheet replacing the head. As a second member was returning, a voice was heard to say … "Don't frighten me" … the apparition then disappeared.

It was later confirmed that the wreckage was indeed that of the German Heinkel bomber; that had crashed on the Snowdonia Mountain Range in North Wales, in 1941 and it the process decapitating the Flight Engineer on impact.

That explained the chilling appearance of the ghostly uniformed figure with a plastic bag or small sheet in place of the head … the Headless Ghost of Snowdonia.

WAS IT A WARNING?

On 29th January 2010, Mister Sol Hafeez contacted me with a very interesting story; so much so – with knowing Samlesbury airfield in Lancashire and the area from where the ghostly incident came from – I have removed a story and included Mister Hafeez's interesting story in Ghost Stations™ The Story.

During the war years many aircraft were built at Samlesbury; the main ones being the twin engined Hampden bombers and the four-engined Halifax bomber. The area was also home for English Electric who set their roots at Warton; and it was mainly at Warton where I did my research for my English Electric Lightning and Canberra books. I did pay many visits to the Samlesbury; and indeed, saw all sites.

So, let me now continue with Mister Hafeez's story. By good fortune, Sol put pen to paper whilst the incident was still crystal clear in his mind. So, told exclusive to me; here is Sol's ghostly story:

"I am employed as a Security Officer and currently working on the British Aerospace site at Samlesbury in Lancashire.

"British Aerospace are currently constructing three huge hangars for assembling fighter jets. The Site of these hangars is deep within the old Samlesbury aerodrome complex. They are being built on a large expanse of open land; with the old runway only a stone throw away, and the famous Samlesbury Hall no more than about a thousand metres beyond the ten foot high Security Fence across the fields.

"On Friday 22nd January 2010, last week, I began my twelve-hour night shift at 18-30 hours. I have been sent to this Site to assist an engineer; who has to read and record the temperatures and gas pressures of sensitive machinery, to ensure that they are all operating within their 'Safe Limits'.

"At about 20-00 hours, a very thick fog had rolled in from across the nearby fields.

"At 23-00 hours we walked over to the main hangar to do yet another reading. These trips to the hangars usually take about fifteen minutes and then we return to our respective cabins. These cabins are made of steel and are transportable; portable huts of various sizes. The biggest is the one I stay in which is about thirty foot in length and twelve foot wide.

"There are about eight of these cabins on the Building Site; and the one that I reside in is the last in the line, overlooking the Building Site and the fields.

"Apart from me and the engineer, there are also three other Security Staff; but they are stationed at the main British Aerospace gatehouse about a quarter-of-a-mile away from our Site.

"It was about 23-30 hours when strange things started to happen. I was sitting in my cabin and reading with the radio turned on low volume when there was a huge bang on the roof of my cabin. It sounded like a heavy brick landing on the steel work above. I jumped up and immediately ran outside, absolutely convinced that the engineer, Chris, was playing a practical joke.

"I was shocked to find no sign of anyone. I quickly ran over to his cabin and found him sitting down in deep conversation on his mobile phone. He broke off to find out what I wanted … I asked him if he threw a brick. He persistently denied it. As I was walking back I thought it over and knew it was extremely unlikely that he could have got back to his cabin in time without me seeing him. His cabin is about hundred-and-fifty yards away; also unlikely that he could throw a brick with such an accurate aim from that distance.

"I checked the entire area surrounding the cabins where anybody could have been hiding, but could absolutely no sign of anyone. I dismissed the idea of climbing onto the roof of my cabin. It was a wet, slippery night and this would have been a breach of health and safety; the rules of which are very strict on this particular Site. I would almost certainly lose my job if I had an accident doing so.

"The moment I walked back into my cabin and closed the door behind me, there was three huge bangs on the side of the cabin followed by another loud bang on the roof, as if someone was hitting it with a hammer.

"I immediately ran outside and circled the entire area. Again, no sign of anyone. There was just no way anybody could have escaped so quickly without me seeing them. By now I was frightened. I knew I was encountering something that was possibly supernatural. These banging's continued on and off for another forty-five minutes and every time I ran outside …nothing. No sign of man or animal.

"The final straw came when I returned to the cabin and heard the same banging's but this time just to the right of one of the windows. I rushed over to the window and slid it open, as I did so; a large piece of wet mud went flying past me, with some of this mud sprinkling onto my face. A few seconds later a small stone ricocheted off the glass on the window. I have no idea where the mud or stone came from. Yet again I rushed out to investigate and yet again the entire site surrounding me was in complete silence … Nobody hiding behind any of the cabins playing tricks.

"Then it stopped as suddenly as it started; the stone and mud incident was the last of the night's strange events. The time now was about half-past midnight on 23rd January 2010.

"I have gone over the events in my mind constantly and am convinced that I was visited by a ghost that night. There was no way that it could have been burglars because the Security System on these premises is extremely thorough; as I mentioned earlier, there are ten foot high fences surrounding the entire complex with a state of the art CCTV system in operation. Even if it were burglars, why on earth would they want to draw the attention of Security? Likewise, I cannot possibly see the other three Security Officers on the main gate quarter-of-a-mile across the fields leaving their warm office to play silly jokes and carry it on for nearly an hour on a dirty, wet building site in the dead of night. Nobody could have come right up to the cabin and then escape so fast without me seeing them, believe me it is just not possible.

"The first people to turn up for work in the morning were the two Site Managers. I related the night's happenings to them and was shocked when they told me that other staff working late at night have also experienced the same knockings and banging's and that one or two have actually seen apparitions on the old runway just outside the building site. They said that the famous Lady in White from Samlesbury Hall has also been seen on this runway.

"I did not see any apparitions myself, but I am definitely convinced that this Site is badly haunted after my experience that night.

"As far as I am aware the old runway will remain intact with no plans to build over it; but sadly I will be finishing on this Site in early February 2010. So it is unlikely I will ever find out just exactly who my ghostly visitor was."

Thank you, Sol. A very interesting story and I await with interest what my Readers will say about it.

THE MEMORIAL

Here …
Right here …
Here is where I will stay,
Be it night or be it day.
Here …
Right here …
Here is where I will stay,
As I remind of the many a dark day.
Here …
Right here …
Here is where I will stay,
Representing those in foreign fields that lay.
Here …
Right here …
Here is where I will stay,
A symbol of keeping evil at bay.
Here …
Right here …
Here is where I will stay,
In rain, snow or basking in sun's golden ray.
Here …
Right here …
Here is where I will stay,
Showing the great cost man had to pay.
Here …
Right here …
Here is where I will stay,
Please do not ignore me I pray.
For here …
Yes, right here …
Here for all to see, is where I will stay.
I the Memorial!

Written by Baron Barrymore Halpenny – March 2003

21ST CENTURY INTERVIEW

Maria Grazia

An interesting interview was one, in so much as it was the first I had ever done by way of the Internet, and this was with Maria Grazia of www.true-ghost-story.com, which was on put on their website on April 08, 2009

The Introduction and interview was as follows:

Bruce Barrymore Halpenny is a well-respected British military historian. He is also the author of a series of very informative and highly entertaining books called the Ghost Station Series. These books highlight the chilling mysteries and ghostly occurrences that surround wartime airfields in the United Kingdom.

Join us today for an interview with author Bruce Barrymore Halpenny as he recounts the early inspiration for the series and ponders upon the reason why these locations hold so much ghostly energy.

Would you tell us a bit about your writing background and experience in the realm of the supernatural?

How I got into writing in the first place I explain fully in my book stated at Q7 so will only briefly do so here. I will just say that I was the first and only one to fully examine; record and fully research airfield supernatural activity and so understandably became the acknowledged expert in this field. I still get a great many letters and e-mails – all most welcome I might add – from people from around the world interested in this amazing and yet so misunderstood, fascinating subject. One, who thinks a Time Zone is possible, is Lord Balfour. During an **Exclusive** Interview with me, he said: "Everyone cannot be wrong who claims to have seen a ghost. And, I feel quite sure that it is the case, that there are various persons, who meet with some terrific situation, or shock, to leave in the ether, a memory, of what they have been through, and this is interpreted, rather like we interpret the waves of wireless and television.

"If a suitable receiving mind comes in contact with the impression left by the individual in the case, there is the ghost. Who would have thought the ether held waves interpreted by television now today in hundreds of different ways."

Science I still maintain, do not have the tools or the people with the right 'open-minded' approach to understand sensibly or fully research this subject.

When I started my research into airfield histories I quickly found that virtually no records were kept and some that were available were so sparse that they were next to useless. Much of this did not surprise me as I had encountered this during my Service in the RAF, for my orders were to destroy all records on bases that we were closing. The only course available to me was to do the research myself and though this cost a vast amount of time, energy and money, which has never been recouped to this day, it did allow me to know the airfields inside out.

My research connected with my knowledge from my Military Service, has given me an unrivalled knowledge of the airfields and the men and women who served on them. As I amassed such knowledge and information, I also acquired airfield supernatural stories and began to research these, in order to find the answer to the reason.

My special knowledge and know-how to open all doors is made abundantly clear in the Lightning XS894 Mystery in the New Edition – (October 2008) of my Ghost Stations™ Mysteries, when Pat Otter of the Grimsby Evening Telegraph and his top aviation friend from Northcliffe Newspapers – all stated in my book on pages 47 & 48 – had all doors slammed in their faces when they started to ask questions. Only I can open the doors, as my Readers are fully aware.

What inspired the excellent Ghost Stations series of books?

The ghost/supernatural and unexplained events came about with my research for the airfields for articles I did in the Sixties and Seventies and later in my books in the Action Stations Series that I did. These being AS2 Military Airfields of Lincolnshire and the East Midlands, AS4 Military Airfields of Yorkshire and AS8 Military Airfields of Greater London. This was the true start for the Ghost/Supernatural stories; and I had a vast number of stories ... literally hundreds. So I took them all very seriously and from my vast research we got Ghost Stations™. I thought that was that; but the public thought otherwise and I soon received hundreds of letters asking when was the next Ghost Stations™ book out. So I had boxes of information that I put to good use, for so many people got so much pleasure from my true ghost/mystery stories; and ... out came GS2 ...then GS3, then GS4, GS5, GS6, GS7, and last but not least Ghost Stations™ 8.

My unique experiences in the military aside, I found the more I researched into the airfield histories and the more I interviewed RAF and Army and Navy personnel – Men and Women - both serving and retired, the more I encountered ghost stories and stories of supernatural events that could not be fully explained. I do explain this in my book due out in June 2009 that covers my

Special Military Service. I am now working also on that book and it does bring back many happy memories.

What was the most frightening story told to you for the series? Or at least one of the most frightening stories?

There are several; and everybody loves a Ghost story. They are all frightening at first; but not frightening once you know the reason. The Metheringham Lass™ is the most chilling experience for those that encounter it. That story is in Ghost Stations™ 1 and also in Ghost Stations™ Lincolnshire. Another is The Cottesmore Ghost in Ghost Stations™ 3.

What was one of the most touching stories told to you?

All my stories are touching in one way or another because one can tell that they are true ghost, mystery stories. Being all my life with dogs; and that includes also when in the Military I had the most feared dog of the Military; that being Air Dog Blaze. So I love the two about the dogs; Ming The Faithful in Ghost Stations™ 1 and Bobby's Vigil also in Ghost Stations™ 1, but one, which I called The Canteen Ghost in Ghost Stations™ 1, was very moving, for Mollie Tilley was in tears telling me. She was so sincere and very genuine.

The list is endless, but another to touch a soft spot is The Last Goodbye in Ghost Stations™ 1. Mrs Meeson a lovely Lady that brings a tear or two to your eye. I like and had great pleasure to research the Message From The Air in Ghost Stations™ 1.

One must not forget, The American Phantoms at RAF Kimbolton in Ghost Stations™ 1. A big, big cover-up with that story. And talking of cover-ups and Yanks must just mention: Lightning XS894 Mystery. I was first with that and also with The Harrier Jet Mystery, both these stories are in the new Ghost Stations™ Mysteries.

What is it about airfields that draws so much ghostly energy?

That is easy to explain. The airfield held so many people, at any given time on average just over 5,000 in such a small place for such a short period of time in terms of history, and yet many of these aircrew had violent deaths having been only a short while ago, safe and sound among friends, then suddenly over enemy territory fighting for their lives. This mode of war was unique for the Royal Air Force who, unlike soldiers or sailors, who are given a little time to acclimatise themselves to this new situation of kill or be killed; whereas, one minute the bomber crews are safe in the Mess at an airfield in Lincolnshire or Yorkshire and in under the hour entering hostile territory on the way to bomb Berlin. It is – unless you were there – impossible for one to comprehend the fear and the tension.

The mind and body does not get a chance to adjust; and, I speak from experience from just my special duties in the military, for you have to adjust or call it a day. For aircrew it was impossible to adjust due to the fact that on entering the aircraft, you have given up your freedom and now in the hands of not only your crew; but also the aircraft. You now depend on so many other factors to stay alive and get back safely. Lady Luck sure had to be onboard with you.

In the First World War it was Tommy; in the Second World War it was the aircrews that were the cannon fodder. That is the reason why ghost stories abound in and around the old wartime airfields; and why so many Earth bound Spirits are on the old wartime airfields. The human soul has not come to terms with this rapid change, the lies and deceit.

Have you ever witnessed a ghost yourself or have had any encounters with the supernatural?

That is hard to say, for we may all have seen a ghost and yet not realised it. But in the sense of seeing a ghost and knowing that what I am seeing is a ghost, then the answer is no. As for encounters with the supernatural, then yes on several occasions, the ones I recall well, were when I was in the Royal Air Force Military Police (RAFPD) Special Duties – Nuclear and Chemical Weapons.

I have also witnessed a UFO whilst at my home in Abruzzo, Italy. My place at that time was on the mountain with a wonderful view over the Adriatic Sea. At 0200 hours one early January morning I was out looking at the stars when suddenly I noticed a bluish glow on a silver cigar shaped object moving from Pescara along the coast just above the sea, in the direction of Foggia (the heel of Italy). The speed puts it firmly as a UFO for its speed was staggering and I can fully judge an aircraft and its speed, but this was exceptional. Natural phenomena? I do not think so.

Yes many cases can be explained and yes there are hoaxes, some are deliberately orchestrated by governments to discredit the UFO research community, but there are cases and experiences that just cannot be explained away. Yes, there are UFOs as I have proved with my story: LIGHTNING XS894 MYSTERY and pilot Captain Schafner.

It is very hard to say about seeing ghosts, visions, etc, but a classic example is in the story The Four White Parachutes in Ghost Stations™ 3, here Geoffrey Hall saw clearly Four White Parachutes in the sky, but Bert Hawes did not and yet it was to have a meaning.

Would you tell us about any upcoming books?

There are several I am working on, one being: Top Secret - RAF Barnham and I. This is about my military career and the Atomic Storage base RAF Barnham, which to this day is still shrouded in mystery and Ministry of Defence false information. I am writing the book to set the record straight, but I also list several supernatural events that took place whilst I was there and whilst on other Special Duties.

There will be more Ghost Stations™ to follow ….. my readers will see to that.

I pause for a moment to pose for this picture with the 747 that Qantas so kindly gave to me.

A LETTER FROM AN ARDENT FAN

The following letter is just one of the hundreds of Fan letters; and I publish in full said letter, with photocopy of the poem Grace that Duncan refers to in his letter dated 10th September 1993. I have photocopied the said poem from the back of his letter in order to keep it just as he put it.

10th September 1993

Dear Bruce,

I was reading your books for the umteenth time over the last few days, partly because I had just returned from a quick tour around some of the old airfields in Lincolnshire. It was great to see some of the old places again and also to see that even after all these years, mind you it does make one feel ruddy old.

Blyton was the one that had me fooled until I found an old road map that showed that the country lane all overgrown and with trees that I was looking at when I was there used to be the main road as I knew it. It was strange as there is nothing in that exact area to show any buildings had ever been there but as I sat there in my Landrover I got a sort of 'feeling' that I had got the location right. Actually Blyton has one old small AM building that we used to drive through to get to the refuelling point at Kirton Lindsey. I must also confess that I was a little disappointed not to see any phantom airmen or maybe a phantom Queen Mary belting around somewhere, just kidding, it was great, I intend to do another soon around the Yorkshire area, using your book as a guide of course.

The other thing(s) I wanted to ask, any more Ghost Stations, I have No:4. The other thing is about that poem in your WARTIME POEMS book, the one called GRACE.

When I was stationed at Finningly we had some old Wimpey's lined up outside the hangar that was used in part by the MT Section to store the Bross Snow ploughs and other vehicles. That was the hangar next to the one used by 616 Squadron. The two that stood side by side. I didn't take a lot of notice at the time but I think they were being dismantled and taken away by road, sort of bit by bit. Anyway I was on the scrounge, as was my wont, looking to try and obtain by fair or foul means a waterproof cover for my motor-bike, and as these kites had engine covers I was after one.

Curiosity led me to have a look inside one or two of the fuselages and in one I found an oily piece of paper, I think it was an F100 but am not sure, the paper was not in the best of conditions and came apart at the folds but on it was written the same poem, not exactly the same. Anyway I copied it down and have had it in my old pay-book for ages. That paper in turn has now come apart (boy do I feel ruddy old) but I have managed to copy it down, I forgot to do it the last time I read your book but this time I did a search (and in this house I mean SEARCH). You say you know the author; it could be that as with a lot of these poems there is more than one. I'll pop it on the other side of this letter.

I hope that you and yours are well,

CHEERS,

Duncan Gray. (The ship in bottles bod)

THERE WAS NO TITLE.

```
SHE STOOD ALONE,
SHE WAS ONE OF THE BEST,
AND I'D VOWED TO-NIGHT I'D GIVE HER THE TEST.
SHE LOOKED SO LOVELY,SLEEK AND TRIM,
THE NIGHT WAS DARK,THE LIGHTS WERE DIM.
I LOOKED HER OVER WITH MUCH DELIGHT,
BECAUSE I KNEW SHE WAS MINE TO-NIGHT.
I FELT SO EXCITED MY HEART MISSED A BEAT,
I KNEW BY HER LOOKS I WAS IN FOR A TREAT.
I SAW HER STRIPPED,I SAW HER BARE,
MY FINGER TOUCHED HER EVERYWHERE.
I GOT INSIDE HER,SHE SOON SCREAMED WITH JOY,
THIS WAS HER FIRST TIME OUT WITH A BOY.
I GOT UP HIGH AS HIGH AS I COULD.
WE ROLLED AROUND AND BOY SHE WAS GOOD.
 I TURNED HER OVER,RIGHT ON HER SIDE,
THEN ON TO HER BACK AS SHE STARTED TO SLIDE.
AS WE CAME DOWN TO EARTH WITH AN EXTATIC SIGH,
I MARSHELLED MY THOUGHTS JUST TO BID HER 'GOOD BYE'.
MY VERDICT IS,SHE'S THE BEST IN THE LAND,
THAT BRAND-NEW MOSQUITO FOR FIGHTER COMMAND.
```

No name,but I'm glad I found it and kept it all these years.

Duncan gray

118

ONE OF THE REASONS WHY THE OLD AIRFIELDS ARE HAUNTED

I sent Ghost Stations™ 3 to Wing Commander Ken Wallis to ask him to read it; and for his comments on the Z-Men pages 133 - 145.Winco Wallis duly obliged and the following is his full report. The reply of Wing Commander Kenneth Wallis goes a long way to explain one of the Questions put to me in my 21st Century Interview; which is published in this book.

30 August 2008

Dear Barry,

Many thanks for the opportunity to read your further fine publication, 'Ghost Stations 3' and for the chance to comment on 'Z-Men' pages 133 - 145.

I totally agree that there would be the odd lie told to the family of someone who had been killed, to cover up what had really happened. Anyway, it would probably cause the family less grief to think their son had died in action with the enemy, rather than by mistake by his own side.

Also, of course, there might be good reasons in the cause of 'Security' not to reveal what had actually happened.

There is no doubt that, in bombers we were often subjected to 'friendly fire'. We were always shot at when staggering back across the North Sea and we approached Harwich. It almost served as a 'Marker Beacon' to us.

Also, on the way out and flying over the Wash and the North Norfolk coast, before darkness had set in, it was not uncommon to see a string of tracer fired at the out going 'Wellington' by our own ships. I think they were very 'jumpy' and it was natural to them to fire.

I don't think many of the aircrew wanted to fly bombers, I certainly didn't and I was not one of the Lysander pilots who responded to the request for volunteers for bombers.

Like most of us, I found myself 'volunteered' whether I wanted it or not.

When you were on 'Wellingtons' as I was, in the tough times of 1941 and 2, if you were not frightened you must have been incredibly stupid.

However, most of us realised there was a job to be done and you must not appear to be frightened. We all knew full well, after a briefing on the 'Target for tonight' in the afternoon, as we sat around in the Ante-Room after an evening meal, and in civilised conditions, that probably at least about six of us would be dead before morning.

We had an arrangement with friends that they could have my bacon and eggs, in addition to their own, if I did not come back.

I had the extra bacon and eggs on many occasions. I gather they had to cook on the assumption they would all come back, or such rations were provided.

I also so well remember some cases of 'LMF' and the Station Parade in which Aircrew Sergeants were stripped of their Sergeants stripes in humiliation because they were 'chickening out.'

I had an example when I had a new member of my crew for some reason. He completely 'lost it' when we came under a bit of flack near the target, though it was not very hazardous.

We duly reported him on return and I do not know what became of him.

I also had a Bomb-Aimer/Second Pilot in the crew of five in a Wellington X when we flew to Italy via Morocco and Algiers in January 1944.

He was a Sergeant James. He was the only member of my crew that had not done a previous tour of Bomber Ops.

My Navigator F/O Morgan had been very badly burned in a Wellington crash and he bore the scars. He was jolly brave to go back on Ops again. However, we knew we would soon be required back *on Ops so we got together to do so, the 'odd one out' being Sergeant James.*

James apparently 'took to his bed' when we were at Tortorella, with 37 Squadron, near Foggia.

I think we did some of the two trips a night to the Anzio Beach head without him. I do not know what actually happened to him.

He had even been useless on the flight to Italy and had cocked-up changing over the fuel tank taps when we were flying over the Atlas Mountain.

Both engines cut out and it was only prompt action by Flying Officer Morgan, the Navigator, that we got the engines going again before we hit the mountains.

There were undoubtedly many losses due to our own equipment, particularly armament.

I have seen one of our bombers blow up completely, before we reached the target and when we were not subjected to flak.

There were the times when we were first carrying the type 37 Long Delay fuze. A glass ampoule of acetone would normally be crushed by the 'windmill' on the fuze when the bomb was dropped and it would be detonated after the acetone had softened a celluloid disk holding back the firing pin, thus causing the delay.

However, it is likely that, probably on a rough take off, the glass ampoule would get broken and the bomb would eventually detonate when still on the bomb rack.

As you will know, the Germans soon learned how to recognise a Type 37 fuze in a bomb that had not been detonated on impact.

They soon worked out the likely delay, from the temperature, etcetera and would safely unscrew the Type 37 fuze before it was due to work.

So, we had the bright idea, when we learned of the German experts, to install the 'anti-removal device' on the Type 37.

Of course, if you are screwing something, like a fuze, into a place and it sticks out for some reason, it is a natural reaction to just wind it back a bit.

This happened to quite a few of our own Armourers, it was a natural reaction, though they should have known better!

I gather that when the anti-removal device was suddenly introduced it killed off lots of the German experts.

I have strong memories of the 'Rodded Bombs' we were dropping over the Anzio beachhead. The rod extending some two feet from the nose fuze caused the bomb to detonate above ground, to achieve the maximum anti-personnel effect.

It also wrote off some of our own bombers when the 'stick' of bombs jostled after being dropped and the detonations would go on up to the bomb dropping aircraft.

They also caused many accidents on the ground and I owe my life and of the rest of the crew, to an *observant and brave technician who saw the nose of an armed 250-pound bomb, with its rod extending forwards as it was just retained by the distorted bomb doors that were just holding it up.*

It must have been iced-up at the bomb release, and retained until we came down below the freezing level and it then fell on the bomb doors and the safety fan had been pulled out.

Normally, of course, after taxying in shutting down the engines the bomb doors are selected open to relieve hydraulic pressure.

We were lucky indeed that an observant and very brave technician run towards my Wellington as I was about to shut down, with his arms making the 'Bomb Doors Closed' sign. I wondered why he was 'F...ing about' but we soon saw when we came down the ladder with the bomb doors closed but only just retaining the live bomb.

I have tried many times to find technical information on the 'Rodded Bombs' but with no success. I have no knowledge of them ever being used over Germany and I suspect they many well have been made in Cairo or somewhere.

They were certainly used in North Africa and in Italy. I suspect they did not meet 'The Geneva Convention' or some such.

Regarding some crews deciding to land in neutral territory, such as Sweden, that certainly did go on. I remember how some of our bomber crews 'got lost' and landed in Eire, where they had to remain.

I do not have any memories of the 'Automatic Gun-Laying Turrets' or 'Z-Equipment.' That would have been a bit later than my time on Ops.

Returning to the subject of our own armament causing losses I have very strong memories of the night of the 21st January 1942.

The target was Bremen, for which we had a full bomb-load of small incendiaries. However, it was also to be one of the first experiments, which led to the Pathfinders.

We had a number of 4.5 inch Reconnaissance Flares also on the bomb racks below the incendiaries.

The object was to release the flares so as to light the way from Emden to Bremen for others to follow.

We were at some 19,000 feet and the Navigator went to the Bomb Aimer position and asked: "Bomb doors open" Then it was "Fares gone, bomb doors closed."

He asked the Rear Gunner to say when the flare lit up but the response was "No f...ing flare." So the navigator again ordered "Bomb doors open" and I complied, to be followed by the same "Flares gone, bomb doors closed."

Although I was wearing the necessary oxygen mask I then smell burning and I asked if anyone else could.

There was then a mighty explosion in the bomb bay, which blew the forward plywood bulkhead of the *bomb bay into the cockpit, accompanied by a brilliant white light and filling the cockpit with masses of smoke.*

It was impossible to see the instruments or outside and we were well and truly on fire in the bomb bay and we attracted much flak. I really thought we had had it. I could not even tell what was the right way up!

The navigator then screamed "Jettison, Skipper" I pulled the 'Jettison' knob and the whole blazing mass dropped on the bomb doors and bashed them open.

We were left with the fabric on the underside still burning but we gradually won the battle.

There was a good view of the North Sea from the narrow catwalk to the rear turret.

We got back to base and it was then apparent how much heat was involved. The lower part of the bomb beams were melted but there were still fuel pipelines at the top of the bomb bay and intact.

The cause of the awful experience was very simple. The bomb doors were iced-up and the first flare dropped on them but had not fallen far enough for its time fuze to be activated.

On the second flare dropping the time fuze was started and it was that that I smelt burning. The massive magnesium flare and its parachute were then blown from the 4.5-inch tube, alight and in the bomb bay. The intense heat of the magnesium immediately ignited the incendiary bomb load. If I had not pulled

126

the jettison knob the moment I did it would have been too late.

I guess our deaths would have been put down to enemy action rather than the short comings of our own equipment.

Icing and armament, was certainly the cause of many of our losses. There was no way the crew would know that a Rodded bomb had been retained on the bomb release, only to be dropped on the closed bomb doors after the aircraft descended below the freezing level.

There was no way of knowing the bomb doors were iced-up and not opening when selected open.

I specialised in Armament post WW2 and we were having lots of complaints that the 25-pound Practice Bomb was failing to detonate when it hit the ground or the sea, as when dropped from the Lincolns at Scampton from about 22,000 feet.

I decided it was due to the spring-loaded safety plunger icing up in the bomb and the spring not popping the safety plunger out when the bomb left the rack. It was held in for safety when on the rack.

I write this up and Bomber Command in their wisdom (?????!) decreed that to ensure the plunger was removed when the bomb fell from the rack it was to be attached to the rack by a wire lanyard. This was a disaster waiting to happen; and it did, many times.

When dropped the bombs would be snatched so violently by the iced-up plunger that they would *tumble end-over-end and land short of the 'Danger Area' in Lincolnshire always killing a prize calf worth £500 or some such. I even once had to go to the Prussian Queen Hotel in Theddlethorpe to inspect the ladies loo, where a 25-pound Practice Bomb had gone in the loo while the seat was still warm!*

Sometimes the bomb would be retained in the bomb bay, dangling on the iced-up plunger and the retaining wire, but the crew would not know it had not dropped.

When the Lincoln - or Canberra - descended below the freezing level there was a live bomb laying on the bomb doors just waiting to slide forward and detonate when the brakes were applied on landing.

I came up with an idea to eliminate the safety plunger entirely, with the possibility of easily modifying all Practice Bombs on the Station; but the response to the idea I had submitted, in a drawing and write-up on how it works was:

"The proposal is fundamentally unsound and cannot possibly work."

I was told this by the One Group Armament Officer and he then quietly said: "I know you would not have modified a Service stove without authority, but does it work?

I said it certainly does and the idea was again submitted by One Group.

It was some nine years before the No: 2 Mark 1 Practice Bomb of my design was adopted. I enclose herewith a listing of personnel injured and aircraft damaged in a two years period, while the answer, which abolished the safety plungers entirely, was already available and could have been applied to existing stocks of Practise Bombs.

It was a dreadfully frustrating period; and a story in itself. In the end I received a polite letter and £150.00 for my invention. I had not done it for the money.

I do apologise, Barry, for all this dreadful scribbling - on. It was all aroused by those pages 133 - 145 in your fine Ghost Stations 3, which I have yet to read in detail.

I do wish I had looked at an old O.S. map before my last "Photographic Mission" to Barnham. It would have complied more precisely to your requests. Let me know should a further "Mission" be required.

All the Very Best, Barry.
Yours sincerely
Ken

Thank you Ken. Excellent and I am certain that my Readers will certainly think so; and to help make it clearer I show some pictures on pages 130 and 131.

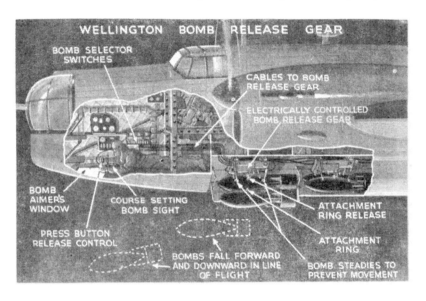

WELLINGTON BOMB RELEASE GEAR

BOMB SELECTOR SWITCHES

CABLES TO BOMB RELEASE GEAR

ELECTRICALLY CONTROLLED BOMB RELEASE GEAR

BOMB AIMER'S WINDOW

COURSE SETTING BOMB SIGHT

ATTACHMENT RING RELEASE

PRESS BUTTON RELEASE CONTROL

ATTACHMENT RING

BOMBS FALL FORWARD AND DOWNWARD IN LINE OF FLIGHT

BOMB STEADIES TO PREVENT MOVEMENT

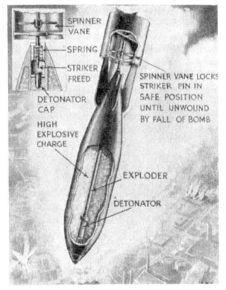

SPINNER VANE

SPRING

STRIKER FREED

DETONATOR CAP

HIGH EXPLOSIVE CHARGE

SPINNER VANE LOCKS STRIKER PIN IN SAFE POSITION UNTIL UNWOUND BY FALL OF BOMB

EXPLODER

DETONATOR

Above shows the bomb release gear and you can see the position of the bombs in relation to the bomb aimer and pilot.
Left is a diagram illustrating how the bombs were supposed to be "safe" until they have been released from the bomb rack, but as you read from Ken, this did not always work

130

I show this picture to give you some idea of a bomb load in the bomb bay though the aircraft shown is not a Wellington, with doors open. Imagine them closed and these bombs fell on them.

BOOK SIGNINGS & INTERVIEWS

In the early days I did a great many book signings and interviews; that were great and very rewarding to meet my many Fans; but very demanding. I returned many times to do a special tour; and one included me speaking to a very, very packed audience in the control tower at the old wartime bomber airfield of Elvington in Yorkshire, that is home for the Yorkshire Air Museum, who invited me. It certainly was a packed house; and a great pleasure to be there.

Another interview was the 21st century interview; and that for me was my first Internet Interview with a charming young lady in Canada. There are many good reasons why I did the interview, one being that I am Irish/Canadian; another that the good lady sent me a photograph and is what you now see, along with the questions she asked and my answers to them. Did you like the 21st Century Interview?

Page 133– Top: Book signing at RAF Cranwell

Page 133 – Bottom: Book signing at Sharples bookshop in Coningsby, Lincolnshire.

Above: Book launch of Action Stations 4 in Yorkshire at RAF Linton-on-Ouse.

Top page 134. Lightning book launch at RAF Binbrook with Baron, keeping hold of the Lightning book.
Bottom page 134. Book launch at RAF Coningsby.

Page 137. Ghost Stations™ book signing at Hillards Super Store on Wragby Road.

From Wing Commander W B Kane RAF

ROYAL AIR FORCE
Wittering Peterborough PE8 6HB
Telephone. Stamford 64501
0780   GPTN   835   Ext 3203

Bruce Barrymore Halpenny

Please reply to The Officer Commanding
Your reference

Our reference
WITT/1721/Org
Date
10   September 1986

RECEIVED 1 3 SEP 1986

Dear Mr Halpenny

Further to Group Captain Millar's letter on 8 September 1986 concerning
arrangements for the launch of your new book GHOST STATIONS I thought you
may be interested to know that last week a Mrs Lillian Gray retired from
service as a civilian working in the Sergeants' Mess after 17 years.
However, in sifting through her previous RAF associations I discovered
that she was actually stationed as a member of the WAAF here at Wittering
during the war between 1941 - 1944.

I noted that you were keen to use the No 1(F) Sqn Spitfire as part of your
promotion. Mrs Gray worked on this actual aeroplane as "plug tester"
during the war and I thought you may be interested in inviting her to your
reception in view of the local interest.

Mrs Gray now lives locally in Barnack at

> 18 Little Northfield
> Barnack
> Stamford
> Lincs

Naturally I have not mentioned anything to Mrs Gray but should you wish to
use this during your visit please let me know.

Yours sincerely

Bernard Kane

Postscript: We cannot now be certain that the
1(F) Sqn spitfire was the actual plane but
only similar type.

Above getting ready for my Interview with Radio Hallam at RAF Finningley.

Top of page 139 – Book signing at Renault in Lincoln.

Bottom picture page 139. Doing an interview with Keith Skues, who lets me have his chair for the picture. I do not remember if this was at Sheffield for Radio Hallam or if at Hull after he had moved from Hallam. I came purposely back from Italy for the interviews.

One of my many afternoon interviews with Dennis McCarthy at BBC Radio Nottingham. It was always a great pleasure to go to BBC Radio Nottingham.

On pages 141 and 142 you see the book launch for my book Aaargh! that was launched at Jackson Shipley's in Lincoln. They did us proud. The Lightning Jet fighter seat that you see the young lady and myself sitting in was five weeks earlier in a Lightning Jet fighter from RAF Binbrook, zooming through the sky faster than the speed of sound. The seat is still complete.

Book signing at Jackson Shipley in Lincoln where my book Aaargh! was launched.

The Author poses in the Lightning seat whilst signing books.
Jackson Shipley had certainly done us proud.

Freezing cold as I pose for a picture with the Lancaster outside of RAF Scampton. I needed this for my article in the Tit Bits when it was a proper general magazine.

ONE WHO WRITES POEMS

Before we get to One Who Writes Poems, that being Barry Goldsmith, I do say in my Introduction that I would start this chapter by making clear the meaning of poetry, from my Elucidation Chapter of my Poem Book that is now on-hold. I am certain you will find the following very interesting.

A great many attempts have been made to explain poetry with little success. Matthew Arnold called it "a criticism of life." Watts-Dunton gave a carefully thought-out definition: "Absolute poetry is the concrete and artistic expression of the human mind in emotional and rhythmical language." Saint Augustine called poetry "Devils wine," and Wordsworth called it: "the breath and finer spirit of finer knowledge." Dr. Johnson defined poetry as "the art of uniting pleasure with truth, by calling imagination to the help of reason."

According to the celebrated English poet and philosopher Samuel Taylor Coleridge, poetry is " a species of composition opposed to science, as having intellectual pleasure for its object and as attaining its end by means of language natural to us in a state of excitement." Goethe wrote: "True poetry is an earthly gospel setting us free, by an inner serenity and outward soothing effect from the burdens of life." William Hazlitt defined poetry in its matter and form, as "natural imagery or feeling combined with passion and fancy. It is the universal language which the heart holds with nature itself."

I mention Hazlitt, for after indulging in an infatuation for one Sarah Walker - his marriage to Miss Stoddard in 1808 was unhappy to say the least and it was dissolved in 1822; and he married a rich widow, and parted from her a year afterwards.

I mention this for my old friend George Ellmore, the greatest Blacksmith in England, was always saying to me that he was looking for a rich middle-aged widow of twenty-one. I show a picture of George - taken by me - in my book, The Avro Vulcan Adventure, on page 30. George was a Master Blacksmith like Vulcan the Blacksmith, hence the reason he is shown in my book about the Avro Vulcan V-Bomber.

Aristotle has said that all poetry, of whatever kind it may be, is a mode of imitation. Man is the most imitative of living creatures, and takes pleasure in seeing things imitated. Imitation is one instinct of our nature; another deeply rooted instinct is love of rhythm and harmony. Poetry has sprung from these two instincts.

Broadly speaking, poetry is the emotional and imaginative interpretation of life. The poet - as you will see in a moment with Barry's poems - goes to the essence of life, penetrates reality, apprehends facts emotionally, and communicates the feelings aroused in him to his listeners/readers. In his interpretation of life emotion and imagination predominate, and he appeals to our feelings and passions through the medium of rhythmical language, the natural speech of excitement.

When man is excited, swayed by feeling or passion, his language - the vehicle by which he expresses his thoughts and communicates them to others - becomes rhythmical, for exalted moods and a state of ecstasy stimulate such language, as in the orators. Thus one of the chief traits of poetry is that it peculiarly affects the imagination and the feelings.

A common idea, the result of experience and reasoning, may be conceived by the poet in such a way as to strike our feelings with peculiar force; or ideas which, though elevated in themselves are familiar to all, may receive new impressiveness from a new and striking way of expressing them.

Grasping the mystery and beauty of things, the poet interprets them in his own individual way, but always stimulated by emotions and aided by imagination. He becomes not only a dreamer after dark, but also a speaker of essential truth. He speaks in rhythm, because, as Browning once said, "his brain beats in rhythm."

But mere rhythmical language does not yet constitute poetry, for impassioned prose is also rhythmical. It is the union between imagination and emotion on the one hand, and rhythm in verse on the other, which constitutes poetry.

So, let us read the poems of 'One Who Writes Poems' and in this case it is my good friend Barry Goldsmith; but first, a little background history to set the scene.

In February 2000 I asked Barry to let me **exclusively** have a brief history; the following is Barry's very interesting reply:

"You asked for a brief history of myself. Well where do I begin? I suppose at the beginning. I was born here in Southampton in March 1935. Due to the war I was six years old before I could begin school. I did my primary and junior schooling at a school close to where I am now living, 'Bassett Green'. I then went on to Swaythling Secondary Modern, which was right at the bottom of our garden where I used to live in Mayfield Road. As you can probably imagine, being that close to school I was nearly always late.

"On leaving school, I began work with the railway at Eastleigh as an office boy in the Carriage and Wagon drawing office. One year later, and unable to get an apprenticeship there, I was apprenticed as a Coach Trimmer with the Hants and Dorset Motor Services. If you do not know already, a Coach Trimmer is the same as an Upholsterer, but making seats etcetera for cars and public service vehicles.

"In 1956 I went into the RAF for my two years National Service. My Reception Unit was Cardington. Whilst there I had to select my trade. I chose the Fire Service, and as I had some service from Civvy Street, I was sent to the RAF Fire Fighting School at Sutton-Upon-Hull to sit a trade test.

"The RAF had just introduced a new section, 'Station Fireman' and apparently I was the first National Serviceman to sit and pass the exam. From Cardington I went to your old stamping ground, Hednesford for 'Square Bashing'. At the end of that, all us tall erks were sent down to Uxbridge for special route-lining drill for a week. We helped line the route in London for the royal visit of King Faisal of Iraq. My first real posting was to Alness in the north east of Scotland. This was a Maintenance Unit of Coastal Command. Whilst there, I was detached for six weeks to Stanmore Park in Middlesex, for a refresher course.

"Back to Scotland for a few more weeks and I was posted to RAF Mountbatten in Plymouth, Headquarters 19 Group Coastal Command. There for about a year, I eventually managed to obtain an exchange posting to RAF Amport near Andover in Hampshire and not too far from home. This was the Headquarters of Maintenance Command and a truly superb camp.

"It was very small and was once the home of the Marques of Winchester. The HQ was situated in the large stately house and we were dotted about through very picturesque grounds. That is where I was demobbed from.

"Although I have never personally experienced anything mysterious or ghostly on any of my stations, there were two places to which I was posted that had an air of eeriness about them in certain places. One of these was RAF Alness on the Cromarty Firth in Scotland. Whilst I was stationed there it was a marine craft unit; but I understand there were Sunderlands there during the Second World War. That part of Scotland seemed to me to be very bleak to say the least, but around the empty hangars and slipways on that camp was nothing short of creepy.

"The other camp which I found rather disturbing at times was RAF Mountbatten, Plymouth. Here the fire section was built at the base of what can only be described as a cliff, on top of which was part of some old fortifications that housed a large water tank.

"Tales went round the camp that this tower was haunted by the ghost of a Second World War Sunderland crew member; but again, I never saw nor heard anything of the ghost myself. All I do know is that on passing this spot on a dark and windy night was rather unnerving, and I wasn't happy until at last in the section with my mates.

"I went back to my trade and to the Auxiliary Fire Service, which I had first joined in 1954. A luck break - or unlucky I sometimes think - secured me a job as a Trimmer with the railway at Eastleigh. This lasted until Dr Beeching wielded his chopper in 1962, and that is how I came to join the Post Office.

"I worked for the Royal Mail in Southampton, as a postman. I gave them nearly 36 years and then retired early in 1997. I had had enough. I have been writing verse ever since I was at school; and this knack, as I call it, came in very useful while with the Royal Mail. I was able to voice the opinions and protests of myself and my workmates in this way without being rude. Well not too rude. I was always able to 'Hit the nail on the head' as they say. My family says that my poems are like stories in verse, which I suppose they are really. I like to think of my poems as short stories as some of them contain anything up to 20 or 30 verses. A lot of my verse has a supernatural theme running through it, including some that I have written about the RAF. I am married with two daughters and have two granddaughters.

"I would also be very interested to learn of any strange tales you may know of concerning the RAF Camps I found myself posted to during my two years service. They are as follows: Cardington, Hednesford, Uxbridge, Stanmore Park, Alness, Kinloss, Plymouth and Amport in Hampshire.

"Thank you once again for giving me some very enjoyable hours of reading and I look forward to more of your books when I can get hold of them."

Thank you Barry. Now my good Fans, I now give you some of Barry's best poems and want you to let me know what you think of them. Also, which one you like best. The Five Poems that Barry Goldsmith penned for Ghost Stations™ The Story, are: Bless 'Em All, To The Men of The Bombers, A Night To Remember; The Air Show and Knights of The Round Table.

TO THE MEN OF THE BOMBERS

Beside a country churchyard wall,
There stands a headstone, plain and small.
And carved beneath its Air Force crest,
I can read who lies there, now at rest.

His name, his rank, engraved with pride,
His service number, and the date he died.
And I thought of the days now long gone by,
When like all the others he'd enlisted to fly.

And I vowed there and then that my tribute I'd pay,
With a pen and some paper in my own simple way.
For he like so many paid the ultimate fee,
Standing up for their values, their country, and me.

Now their deeds are but history, those days are all gone,
But we'll never forget them, their memory lives on.
Written down are their stories that today seem unreal,
Let these words I have written tell the way that I feel.

The time that I served wearing R.A.F. blue,
Was not the same time as the time served by you.
For mine, though enforced by the same country's law,
Was two years of peace and not six years of war.

Yet I have still shared in your every thought,
In the books I have read of the battles you fought.
When you ate in the Mess I was there at your side,
When you boarded the crew bus I was there for the ride.

I was there as you waited to get the green light,
As you thundered away and soared off in the night.
When you thought of your loved ones tucked up warm as toast,
Down below in their beds as you crossed England's coast.

I was there with your skipper aged just twenty-three,
As he hurried you onwards out over the sea.
I was there with the gunners when they tested their guns,
I was there when they searched the black night for the Huns.

I was there when the searchlights caught you over the Rhur,
And you wondered if this was to be your last tour.
When the flak burst around you and filled you with dread,
I was there when uneasiness entered your head.

And that rattling sound which you said was "Just cack",
As the shells burst outside with an ominous 'crack!'
And I saw the sad looks and the tears in your eyes,
When some of your squadron were blown out of the skies.

When you lost the port inner I felt it go too,
And I ducked with you all as the shrapnel tore through.
And like you I was all for a hasty retreat,
When the next shell exploded beneath the crew seat.

But you and the rest never thought once to stop,
And in less than a moment you'd feathered the prop.
And your course never wavered, you still carried on,
You would not feel happy 'til the bombs had all gone.

Through great jagged holes blew an icy cold blast,
Then the thud as the bomb doors were opened at last.
I could feel the sweat trickling down inside your mask,
As you lay at your bomb-sight intent on your task.

And I felt the plane lurch as the bombs fell away,
Then the skipper banked over and you sped on your way.
And I gazed with you all as you watched the bombs go,
Plunging earthward to fuel the inferno below.

As you made your way homeward, the skipper had said,
"Keep your eyes peeled for the fighters ahead!"
And I hunched over Browning's in the freezing cold tail,
As you silently prayed that your guns wouldn't fail.

And I prayed as you prayed, much harder than most,
To the Father and Son and of course 'Holy Ghost'.
Then in came the fighters speeding out of the night,
And you hammered the leader as he filled up your sight.

But the others peeled off and came in from the beam,
While the tracer came at you as if in a dream.
And I flinched as your plexiglass canopy burst,
And the canon shells hit you and did of their worst.

I was there with you skipper and I saw how you fought,
As you corkscrewed to starboard then corkscrewed to port.
When the instruments shattered all over the place,
And you took the full force of it right in the face.

Half blinded, you struggled to keep the plane straight,
But already you sensed it was probably too late.
With the bomb aimer's help and the column held tight,
You coaxed the plane on through the bitter cold night.

I was there when you told everybody to jump,
And I know at the time in my throat rose a lump.
For three of the crew would be staying inside,
In their battle positions where each one had died.

And you held to your course 'til you knew all had gone,
But you and the bomb aimer still struggled on.
I was there when the mid-upper took to his chute,
When his canopy blossomed he lost his left boot.

I was there on the ground where all was so still,
And I saw the plane turn and dive into the hill.
I had seen quite enough I could no longer look,
And I turned the page over and closed up my book.

The years now have passed, and I'll often go,
To see the old aircraft in museum or show.
And I think of the young men who made up each crew,
Resolute and determined, like brothers they flew.

Then I think of the ones, who gave yesterday,
That people like me might still have today.
And I'll gaze at the sky, all alone in the crowd,
And I'll see Air Force wings etched in every cloud.

B.J.G March 30TH 2000

Barry Goldsmith during his period in the RAF

A NIGHT TO REMEMBER

See the old school building with its windows boarded up,
See the playground where no longer children play.
Now it is the home of the part time Fire Service,
With appliances now painted wartime grey.

Here, the men in charge are full time firemen,
Whose job it is to train the A.F.S.
To make sure they all know what they are doing,
And to do it without getting in a mess.

They must teach them how to run a hose out,
How to operate a trailer pump with speed.
They must use their many skills and all their knowledge,
To pass on the expertise that they will need.

The Auxiliaries have been thrown in at the deep end,
They are going to get a baptism of fire.
As yet they are not aware of just what's coming,
Will they stand, or will they waver and retire?

Some say the A.F.S. are army dodgers,
'Aunt Fanny's Soldiers' who do not want to fight.
They say they are a waste of time and money,
Maybe they'll sing a different tune tonight.

Inside the school it's quite a different story,
The A.F .S. and regulars get on well.
They work together like a band of brothers,
Who'll come out fighting when they hear the bell.

These men now suddenly thrown together,
They have all of them responded to the call.
Shopkeepers, clerks and city bankers,
Are united in their efforts one and all.

It is evening, and the darkening streets are silent,
The drills are over for another day.
The men, uneasy, laugh and talk together,
They are ready for whatever comes their way.

Some are sitting fully dressed and nervous,
Some are playing cards or maybe darts.
One is at the piano knocking out a ragtime tune,
But all can feel the pounding of their hearts.

One stands alone outside in contemplation,
The foremost of his many thoughts is, 'Why?'
And he gazes at the searchlights probing fingers,
As they trace their silvery patterns across the sky.

It is early in September 1940,
Will they get what other towns have called 'The Blitz'.
Will tonight be the first of many without sleeping,
Will they only get their rest in starts and fits?

The control room phones are manned by A.F.S. girls,
At the first ring one girl gives a startled cry.
It's the call to say a heavy raid is coming,
It is time to get geared-up, for standing by.

It won't be long, the distant siren's wailing,
Followed closely by the one just down the street.
And the firemen are buckling belts and axes,
And pulling boots and leggings on their feet.

Above the caterwauling siren comes a new sound,
The drone of heavy bombers can be heard.
And the piano player goes back to his piano,
With his helmet on his head he looks absurd.

Things then begin to happen very quickly,
As the distant thud of bombs draws ever near.
The moment they've all tensely been awaiting,
Is upon them as the phones ring loud and clear.

A firewoman calls in through the doorway,
"Heavy pump to Wilson's, Dockside Lane."
And she jumps back as the crew leaps into action,
While the telephones ring frantically again.

With the firemen now all aboard the appliance,
The driver swings it smartly through the gate.
As the men behind cling tightly to the ladder,
They can only keep their fingers crossed and wait.

As they speed towards the city's busy dockland,
The sky ahead has a lurid orange glow.
With incendiaries falling all around them,
Just what waits, those firemen do not know.

All through the city streets are burning buildings,
Other firemen battle hard, they must not wane.
Onward through the blazing city centre,
That glow ahead, it must be Dockside Lane.

This area of dockland has warehouses,
And it's plain to see they have taken quite a whack.
Smoke and flame is pouring out of windows,
Not only at the front but also at the back.

Immediately the crew goes into action,
Taking water, like the others, from the main.
They know that if they don't get reinforcements,
All their hard work is going to be in vain.

Wilson's is a fair sized shipping chandlers,
The top two floors and roof are blazing well.
While the firemen attack the conflagration,
They have to tolerate its toxic smell.

The water on the firemen's coats is steaming,
The heat is so intense it sears the eye.
And all the time the planes above keep coming,
There are hundreds of them up there in the sky.

The stifling air is full of burning embers,
That the up draught from the fire blows all about.
Then a building near collapses without warning,
There wasn't even time to yell, "Look Out!"

Dust and smoke conceal just what has happened,
As the building bowed and fell into the street.
It crushed a trailer pump and three A.F.S. firemen,
With no warning there was no time to retreat.

Up the road, the crew at work on Wilson's,
Know nothing of this dreadful accident.
Their minds are set on trying to save their building,
To put the fire out is there intent.

For hours they have grappled the inferno,
They have been here hard at work since seven o'clock.
When all at once a deafening huge explosion,
Comes from somewhere just beyond the burning dock.

The water from the hoses stops abruptly,
It is obvious that the water main has gone.
A new supply, it must be found and quickly,
The fight to quench the fires, it must go on.

"Get the water from the river," comes the order,
And the pumps are quickly set up on the quay.
Relaying vital water to the waiting firemen,
Exhausted now, as anyone can see.

More crews arrive to aid the fire-fighters,
They are needed like they've never been before.
Having fought their way across the shattered city,
Some have travelled over forty miles or more.

All through the night the weary firemen battle,
They do not flinch, they never once give in.
As dawns first early light breaks on the skyline,
It is plain to see; at last they are going to win.

By half past six the worst of it is over,
A large part of the dockside has been saved.
And a welcome sight, a van with tea and biscuits,
Appeared like magic, how those firemen waved.

It is time now to pick up the used equipment,
To roll up miles of stiff and blackened hose.
As the firemen mucked in and pulled together,
From the rubble wisps of smoke still slowly rose.

The time has come, they are sent back to their station,
They are worn out by their task, but worst of all,
They have to pass the spot where hours earlier,
A pump's crew disappeared beneath a wall.

Amid the mound of rubble men are searching,
While others, stunned and silent, only stand.
One stoops, and pulls something from the debris,
He has a badly dented helmet in his hand.

Our crew moves on out into the city,
A pall of dust and smoke hangs over all.
Everywhere is snaking hose just like spaghetti,
With brick and glass from many a shattered wall.

But life goes on, the city is awakening,
The milkman and the postman does his round.
As the people all emerge from where they sheltered,
They are dazed and speechless; they do not make a sound.

At last they reach their longed for destination,
And slowly disembark from their machine.
As they make their weary way into the rest room,
Someone asks them how their night has been.

But an answer's going to be a long time coming,
The look upon their faces says it all.
They sink upon their beds from sheer exhaustion,
And even on the floor against the wall.

Last night was just the tip upon the iceberg,
They know they'll have to face a great deal more.
But they'll give it all they have or go down fighting,
If that is what it takes to win their war.

And the people in the streets, who called them Dodgers,
Now buy them tea and cigarettes and beer.
And they say a prayer for them in church on Sunday,
And sometimes, sadly have to shed a tear.

And when the final 'All Clear' has been sounded,
Then the people will remember them with pride.
And maybe they will erect a monument,
An Auxiliary and a Regular, side by side.

B.J.G. November 11th 1997.

The Air Show

THE AIR SHOW

Somewhere in Southern England on a morning in July,
A solitary figure gazed thoughtfully at the sky.
His thoughts his own, he casually lit a cigarette,
And told himself his flight today had to be the best one yet.

Mike was a Spitfire pilot, the year was 1993,
And he owned and flew his aircraft at shows for all to see.
In its standard wartime camouflage of irregular brown and green,
This well-loved Mark five Spitfire was the finest to be seen.

Mike had flown at numerous Air Shows and Battle of Britain
days,
While the crowds below had looked on high with a fond
nostalgic gaze.
Each time he flew, he felt that he was part of his machine,
But today he felt uneasy, what could this feeling mean?

All day long the massive crowd had watched with wondrous awe,
They videoed and photographed nearly everything they saw.
There were displays of aerobatics and helicopter flights,
Fast jets streaking overhead giving many people frights.

Later in the afternoon while the show was in full swing,
Mike stood beside his Spitfire and stroked its curving wing.
In less than thirty minutes now he would take off with a roar,
And that faithful Merlin engine would thrill the crowd once more.

"And now," said the announcer, "A survivor of the few,
Mike Allen's Mark five Spitfire, from 1942."
He then went on to give the details and the history of the plane,
While Mike took off and circled, then flew by low again.

All eyes were glued upon him as he stunted way up high,
Conditions were just perfect, not a cloud was in the sky.
He soared, he weaved, he climbed, he dived, he did a victory roll
With baited breath the crowd below applauded, every soul.

The sun streamed in the cockpit as he climbed up in the blue,
And he had the strangest feeling that chilled him through and
through.
He realised he'd climbed too high, out of sight now of the crowd,
So he rolled the Spitfire off the top and found himself in cloud.

Just where this cloud had come from he couldn't understand,
He felt the urge to get back down, to lower his wheels and land.
He peered now through the perspex, thick cloud was all around,
When suddenly from his radio there came the strangest sound.

A disembodied voice was calling, "Come in! "Come in Red
Two!"
"This is Red leader calling, "Come in! "Come in Red Two!"
No sooner had he heard this than he burst out in the clear,
And found two other Spitfires were beside him now, quite near.

To say that Mike was startled was the truth there was no doubt,
As he tried to gain composure he heard another shout.
"Look out behind, Red leader, you have one on your tail!"
And a dark shape hurtled past him, and a sound like beating hail.

The aircraft nearest to him, exploded in a ball,
Of incandescent fire, and there was nothing left at all.
He flew through all the debris, and below him he could see,
The pieces hit the water where he knew that land should be.

"What the hell was going on!" this wasn't part of the display,
When he got back to the airfield he'd have some things to say.
He tried to use his radio, but answer came there none,
Then a black shape flew straight at him, it came out of the sun.

In panic now he rolled and dived, the blood rushed to his head,
If he'd flown on straight and level, by now he would be dead.
For that shape that flew right at him on a steady even line,
He recognised quite clearly, it was an M.E.109.

He flew down low across the sea and headed for the coast,
He knew he'd soon see Bognor or Selsey Bill at most.
The coastline flashed beneath him as he looked with full intent,
And then it dawned upon him, he was flying over Kent.

He hugged the ground and searched about, but nothing could he see,
There were only fields and meadows where the Motorway should be.
Very soon he'd have to land, his fuel was getting low,
When much to his amazement, there was Biggin Hill below.

He circled once and landed, then taxied to a stop,
And when he saw what happened next, he felt his stomach drop.
A Royal Air Force ground crew surrounded his machine,
They re-fuelled, re-armed and polished it, and wiped the perspex clean.

When he saw the belts of cannon shells stacked upon the floor,
He realised his plane had guns where there were no guns before.
A corporal then approached him and gave a smart salute,
"Your aeroplane is ready, sir, can I help you with your chute?"

No-one seemed to notice the flying suit Mike wore,
Or the helmet he was wearing, he must look strange for sure.
"Get back up there," the corporal said, "And give them one for us,
This time I feel for certain, old Hitler's missed the bus."

Mike started up the Merlin and closed the cockpit hood,
He must get back up in the air, down here was not so good.
His mind was in turmoil as he tried to puzzle out,
Just what it was had happened to turn his world about.

Then like a bolt it hit him, he now began to see,
What he was experiencing was only ever on T.V.
He had found some sort of Time-Warp and flown his plane right through,
This wasn't 1993 it was 1942.

His one thought now was to get back to the only time he knew,
He had to find the doorway and try to get back through.
Mike set his course to where he knew the Air Show ought to be,
And as he neared the area the runway he could see.

He had certainly found the airfield but it didn't look the same,
The hangars and some buildings were wreathed in smoke and flame.
Wheeling round in circles above the airfield high,
Were 109's and Spitfires, their contrails crossed the sky.

166

He had to fly up with them to be above the field,
Taking his courage in his hands, to his maker he appealed.
He kept his eyes wide open as he climbed up in the blue,
But he didn't see the 109 that was climbing with him too.

It was then he saw the tracer bullets shooting past his wing,
And he felt the bang beneath him, and he jumped like anything.
The one thing now he wanted was to leave the plane for good,
So he turned the Spitfire upside down, after sliding back the
hood.

He released the straps that held him securely in his seat,
Fell out, and saw his aircraft disappear beneath his feet.
He was out and tumbling earthwards, when above him came a
crack,
His parachute had opened, he was slowly drifting back.

All the other planes were gone now; the sky was clear and blue,
He had found the Time-Warp doorway and had parachuted
through.
Around him all was quiet as he turned and looked around,
And then he saw his Spitfire as it smashed into the ground.

The Air Show crowd fell silent; they had seen his plane come
down,
It fell on open farmland; it had missed the little town.
Mike Allen landed safely as the ambulance drew near,
When the crowd learned he was O.K. they gave a mighty cheer.

Mike returned next morning, the battered wreck to view,
Only he knew what happened to him up there in the blue.
Tom, his chief mechanic then took him to one side,
He said he had found something, something he should hide.

Tom had gone back to the wreckage when no one was around,
And in the mess that was the cockpit, two cannon shells he'd
found.
"What happened up there Mike?" he asked him looking grim,
But Mike refused to answer, just shook his head at him.

Mike checked the local papers for the year of '42,
He found the date he wanted and read that paper through.
He'd almost given up; he thought his luck was running out,
Then an item on the back page made him give a shout.

It told about a pilot, who at Biggin Hill one day,
Had landed in a Spitfire, dressed in a most unusual way.
He wore multi-coloured overalls and had upon his head,
What they described as a fish bowl, painted white and red.

It said a corporal spoke to him but the man made no reply,
He simply climbed back in his plane, disappearing in the sky.
The Spitfire's serial number, was checked, as was its design,
And they found it was still in pieces on the assembly line.

The article then went on to say, that this Spitfire was shot down,
How it crashed beside the airfield, how the pilot saved the town.
The pilot's burnt and battered body was found inside the wreck,
He was finally identified by his tag around his neck.

He was given military honours, and was buried at the church,
Right beside the airfield, so Mike hadn't far to search.
He found words upon the headstone, with its great big flower-
filled jar,
They were; MICHAEL ALLEN, SQUADRON LEADER,
D.S.O. AND BAR.

B.J.G. March 12th 1996.

168

MY THOUGHTS DURING A RAID

Sergeant John Wright. Taken at Van Ralty Studios, Nottingham.

Sergeant John Wright was educated at High Pavement Grammar School in Nottingham, England. At the age of 18 he was conscripted into the Royal Air force; for he had been a member of the Air Training Corps.

After his training he qualified as an air-gunner and was posted to North Africa in June 1944 to No: 24 Squadron. In July 1944 the squadron moved to Pescara in Italy and Sergeant John Wright was a tail-gunner in Marauders on bombing missions from Pescara.

In August 1944 Sergeant John Wright was transferred to the newly formed No: 30 Squadron, SAAF; and he flew as a tail-gunner in Marauders until the date he was killed in action on 11 January 1945. He was age 20 and was on his 47th mission when their aircraft bought it.

"As far as I know this is the only poem he wrote. It was amongst his effects returned with his flight log by the RAF," said Keith Wright, the brother of Sergeant John Wright.

MY THOUGHTS DURING A RAID

I feel so lonely sitting there
And I can only sit and stare
Whilst sailing Thro' these Angry Skies
And scrutinise with intent eyes
For sign of roving Hun.

At last our objective is here
Observer's voice sounds loud and clear
Bombs armed and fused, left, left steady
Bomb door open all is ready
Then all our bombs rain down.

I feel so helpless sitting there
And I can only sit and stare
At little angry puffs of flack
Which send cold shivers up my back
The while I sit and pray.

I pray to God that if I die
That I will never have to lie
In agony and cold suspense
Suffering pain and more torments
Up in those angry skies

I feel so happy sitting there
Although only to sit and stare
For having crossed over Front Line
And everyone is feeling fine
And all their fears are gone.

One more sortie done
One more battle won
Against my awful fear
That death was much too near
And all is well again,

John Wright, Sgt. SAAF
(Killed in Action
11 January 1945 - aged 20)

The above picture taken at the Ancona Military Cemetery in Italy. February 1945.

COLONEL THOMAS BLOOD

Thomas Blood - commonly called Colonel Blood - was born in Ireland about 1616; and passed away in London in 1680. He was a disbanded officer of Oliver Cromwell; and, lost some estates in Ireland at the Restoration.

Colonel Blood's whole life was one of plotting and adventure; though I am certain that he acted a double part, by keeping the government informed of as much as might secure his own safety and gain favour.

Colonel Blood became famous when he attempted to steal the Crown Jewels; but this I am certain was staged and all will become clear in a moment. First let see the other players in this audacious attempt to steal the Crown Jewels.

John Evelyn (1620 - 1706) English diarist was a friend of Pepys. Evelyn travelled widely and visited various parts of the continent that included Belgium, Holland and France. He had inside knowledge of the politics of his day; and he was also knowledgeable in law; for after completing his course at Oxford, he studied law at the Middle Temple; and in 1659 prepared the way for the Restoration.

This was the re-establishment of the Stuart Monarchy in England in 1660, when Charles II ascended the throne. In 1658 Cromwell passed away after five years rule as Protector. It was because of Evelyn's vast political knowledge why Colonel Thomas Blood had to meet him.

John Evelyn had by 1652 settled at Sayes Court, Deptford, and it was there in March 1671 that he met Colonel Blood; who just two months later on 9th May 1671 made an attempt to steal the Crown Jewels from the Tower of London. This I am certain was obviously staged, for Colonel Thomas Blood was seized with the Crown Jewels in his possession; and despite that fact, Colonel Blood was not only pardoned by the Merry Monarch King Charles II, he also obtained forfeited Irish estates of £750 annual value. Very strange and the Merry Monarch had obviously done a deal with Colonel Blood.

The restored king became known as the Merry Monarch; but whereas the Protector had successfully striven to improve his country's commerce and to conquer her enemies, the reign of the Merry Monarch is one of the most discreditable chapters in English history … that is, until now with Blair and Brown's gang in the 21st Century. Labour would not have done a deal with Colonel Blood; they would have put him in charge.

MAJOR, THE EARL OF ANCASTER, K.C.V.O., T.D.

Gilbert James, 26th Lord Willoughby de Eresby, 3rd Earl of Ancaster. Born 8th December 1907. Educated: Eton, Magdalene College Cambridge (MA). Served in the Second World War 1939-1945: Battery Commander, 153rd Leicestershire Yeomanry Field Regiment R.A., T.A., and Major RA (Wounded, Mentioned in Despatches).

Lord-Lieutenant of County of Lincoln, 1950-1975, MP C Rutland and Stamford 1935-1950, summoned to the Upper House of Parliament as Baron Willoughby de Eresby, 1951., Lord Great Chamberlain of England, 1950 - 1952. JP 1937, CC 1950, Alderman, 1954 Kesteven.

Has been chairman of the BLESMA (British Limbless Ex-Service Men's Association) National Appeal Committee since its formation in 1948 and since 1956 has been National President.

Brief Military History - In 1929 joined the Leicestershire Yeomanry which dates from the year 1794 and was in fact the Territorial Army manned by the local gentry as officers with many of the Senior N.C.O.'s from the First World War and recruits taken mainly from local farms. This consisted of three squadrons A, B, C and Headquarters.

With the war clouds gathering over Europe the Regiment was expanded to full War Establishment. Just after the outbreak of war on the 22nd September 1940 the Regiment moved to Rufford Abbey and the role of the Regiment changed to that of Divisional Cavalry of the 1st Cavalry Division. On the 25th September the first eighty horses arrived and by the end of October this figure had risen to 513.

Then on November 25th the War Office announced that all un-brigaded Regiments were to be converted into Royal Artillery. A choice of gun was allowed, medium, field or anti-tanks; the officers were unanimous in their choice of field.

It was also decided that out of the Regiment there should be formed two Field Regiments Royal Artillery - the 153 and 154, known respectively as "The 153 (Leicestershire Yeomanry) Field Regiment RA" and "The 154 (Leicestershire Yeomanry) Field Regiment R.A."

Major Lord Willoughby de Eresby who by now was well liked amongst the men, not only as an officer but also as a soldier, went with the 153rd and was in command of 'A' Battery with its 4.5 howitzers at Wainfleet. The Regiment had a large piece of coastline to cover, between Boston and Skegness, in the event of any invasion.

In April 1940 the two Regiments separated. The 154 Field Regiment went on active service in the Middle

East while the 153 Field Regiment stayed in the U.K. and in November 1943 the Regiment was converted to an S.P. Regiment, with 25-pounders on a Sherman chassis.

On the 29th June 1944 the Regiment landed in Normandy by means of an American tank landing craft.

After many weeks of bitter hand-to-hand fighting the Regiment was attacked by 9th S.S.Panzer Division on the 3rd August 1944 in the Beaulieu-Maisoncelles area. The Major was supporting the 2nd Irish Guards and was helping an officer get his 'F' Echelon through to the position at La Marvindiere which was cut off and short of ammunition. He agreed with the officer that he must attack the Panther, a 43 ton monster and considered as one of the Germans best tanks, which was crossing the road and that to do so, dismount his .30 Browning, and spray up and down the road to get through. But the Germans mortared the road heavily and for protection he got himself under the Irish Guardsman's tank, which then moved to get a better view of the Panther and in so doing pinned the Major's legs under the track. With the engine running the tank commander could not hear his cries and twenty minutes of hell followed while he lay with his feet pinned trying to give himself morphia and knowing all the time that the tank would reverse the length of the track before his legs would be free.

Eventually he was extricated and with the help of the M.O. evacuated the next morning. This was just before the famous Battle of the Falaise Gap.

176

Note: The Falaise fighting is mentioned in 'Fallen Angels of Death' a true World War Two escape story by Bruce Barrymore Halpenny.

Major The Earl of Ancaster, K.C.V.O., and T.D.

*The Earl of Ancaster in Full Dress Uniform of the
Leicestershire Yeomanry – Portrait by Sir John Merton, R.A.
The uniform is Blue, the chest decorated with Gold and Silver
Braid and Chain Mail on the shoulder. The trousers have a
double Red Band on the outside leg. Boots with swan-neck
spurs are worn with this uniform. The Helmet is blue with a
large white and small red plume attached with Silver mounts.
The sabre completes the dress.*

180

Above we see a contented and happy Lord Ancaster – starting to laugh after what I had just whispered to him – about to shake hands with a director of Barrett; who had loaned me their helicopter for three days.
The two photographs on page 179 are taken with Lord Ancaster at his Family home at Grimsthorpe Castle, during our walk around with Napoleon.
On page 180 Baron seen at the back of the Castle. The bottom photograph is in Lord Ancaster's private room where no-body goes ... only us. That is the first-time a photograph of his private room has been shown to the public.

KNIGHTS OF THE ROUND TABLE

The man came home feeling tired and weary
He took out his key and he opened the door,
He put down his hat and his coat and his briefcase
And found a toy army scattered over the floor.

He tiptoed inside very carefully treading
So as not to decapitate rider or horse,
When suddenly turning he trod on a soldier
And broke it in two with considerable force.

Slowly he bent down and picked up the pieces
And gazed at them lying there in his hand,
Perhaps he could mend it, he couldn't discard it
This wasn't the way his evening was planned.

A long time ago he'd been given the soldiers
One Christmas or birthday when he was a boy,
And to see them like this he was filled with emotion
His face wreathed in smiles and his heart full of joy.

The soldiers belonged now to his young son Michael
Upstairs in the bath getting ready for bed,
And the man then thought back to the days of his childhood
As he looked at the hollow-cast figures of lead.

Down on his knees now he gently retrieved them
Placing them back in their box with such care,
Then taking the lid, just before he replaced it
He looked at the picture confronting him there.

'KNIGHTS OF THE ROUND TABLE', in big bold red letters
King Arthur and Merlin and all of the knights,
And he thought of the games and the battles he'd played in
The jousting, and all of those marvellous fights.

He then laid the box gently down on the table
And searched for the tube of some strong Super-Glue,
Then he carefully mended the soldier he'd broken
The one accidentally broken in two.

Just at that moment his little son Michael
Dashed into the room to kiss him goodnight,
And he said he was sorry for breaking the soldier
But Michael just hugged him and said, "That's alright".

Michael's mother came in and said, "Off up to bed now,
I'll read you a story if you're very good,"
Then she said to her husband, "Before we have dinner,
Have a short nap on the couch dear, I should".

The man laid the box on the couch there beside him
Caressing the figures that lay there inside,
As he thought once again of the days of his childhood,
Tears welled in his eyes and he lay back and sighed

Beside him there, Lancelot, Merlin and Arthur
Knights in full armour with broadsword and mace,
Jousters and bowmen and soldiers in chain mail
Each with a hand painted smile on his face.

Slowly the man on the couch closed his eyelids
Two minutes later he was soundly asleep,
And he dreamed he was near to the castle of Camelot
With King Arthur's standard flying proud on it's keep.

And that painted lead army with its fine prancing horses
The bowmen all wearing their green and brown smocks,
They all came together with battle flags flying
And lifted the lid and climbed out of their box.

Arthur and Lancelot rode on ahead now
Climbing a hillside, a cushion in green,
While Merlin mysteriously appeared on another one
And the army spectacularly rode in between.

The Knights in their helmets with their shields and their lances
Dipped in salute as they proudly rode by,
But Merlin was raising his arms to the ceiling
Up to the ceiling which now was the sky.

As one that bold army turned round and retreated
By an antimacassar all crumpled like rocks,
And then just as noiselessly as they had left it
They all of them clambered back in the box.

The man on the couch now was slowly awakening
But one thing he really could not understand
Why was he cuddling a great big green cushion?
And why did he have Merlin there in his hand?

He picked up the box, that box of toy soldiers
And took it upstairs to young Michael in bed,
Placing it gently at the foot of the bed there
He turned out the light and then kissed Michael's head.

He tried to be quiet as he crept from the bedroom
He tried very hard not to waken the lad,
But as he softly stepped out onto the landing
A voice from the darkness said, "I DO LOVE YOU DAD."

B.J.G. January 15th 1996.

184

WHAT IF …?

In Athens in 317 there were 21,000 male citizens of adult age, 10,000 resident aliens and 400,000 slaves that indicates her material prosperity.

However, the enormous and increasing number of slaves in the end destroyed the basis of freedom, for industry was despised, and all but a small section of the citizens became 'poor whites', to use a modern term.

GLOSSARY

AAC	Army Air Corps
AAF	Auxiliary Air Force
AC	Aircraftman
Amidships	at or towards the middle line of a ship; between stem and stern
AFS	Advanced Flying School
ATC	Air Training Corps
Aussies	People from Australia
BBC	British Broadcasting Corporation
Bods	Military slang for people.
CCTV	Close Circuit Television
CIA	Central Intelligence Agency.
CO	Commanding Officer.
Culham	The place where nuclear scientists in 1988 achieved a world record temperature of 100 million degrees Centigrade; which is ten times hotter than the sun.
Fatigues	Military work distinct from the exercise of arms.
FIDO	Fog Investigation and Dispersal Operation.
Fizzer	RAF slang for charging an airman on Form 252.
Hackles	erectile hairs along the neck and back of a dog.
HAS	Hardened Aircraft Shelter.
HCU	Heavy Conversion Unit.
HQ	Headquarters.
Inkling	a hint.
JT	Junior Technician.

K.C.V.O.	Knight Commander of the Royal Victorian Order.
MP	Military Police.
MT	Motor Transport.
Mossie	Mosquito aircraft.
NCO	Non Commissioned Officer.
NAAFI	Navy, Army, Air Force Institutes.
OSS	Office of Strategic Service - the fore-runner of the Central Intelligence Agency - the CIA.
Piracy	Infringement of Copyright
Pirate	1) To take without permission
	2) An infringer of Copyright
	3) A High-Seas robber
Poetry	Creative thought. The art of expressing the imagination and feelings in metrical form.
Poles	People from Poland. Polish.
RAFPD	Royal Air Force Police Dogs
Red Herring	A false scent to deceive hounds
SAAF	South African Air Force.
SAC	Senior Aircraftman.
Sgt.	Sergeant.
T.D.	Territorial Decoration.
Trick Cyclist	Name given to psychiatrists
Tweeny	A maid-servant who assists as subordinate to two others.
WAAF	Women's Auxiliary Air Force
Wimpey	Wellington Bomber
Winco	Wing Commander
WRAF	Women's Royal Air Force

DOWN MEMORY LANE

The Author poses near the rear turret of a Lancaster bomber; to show just what cramped and lonely conditions the rear-gunner had to endure. It is impossible to imagine spending eight or more hours in a rear-turret. You could not doze off for a second, for the rear-gunner was the eyes to cover the back, above and below the rear of the bomber. The bomber crew depended on the rear-gunner.

Just taking on board the Varsity aircraft my First-Day Nuremberg Covers. This is at the old wartime airfield of Winthorpe on the Lincolnshire/Nottinghamshire boarder. They were franked on the airfield; and that makes them very unique.

Above: The Author at wet and windy RAF Binbrook, and poses in front of a Lightning jet fighter of No: 5 Squadron with sharks eye and mouth painted on front.

Page 190 Top: The Author hard at work and just time to give the camera a glance; before time for more Italian coffee and another cigar.

Page 190 Bottom: The Author working on the English Electric Lightning book; and shown in picture the original English Electric Plan – held by Marian and Baron – that I fetched from English Electric at Warton; along with much other data never before seen and unique Lightning photographs that only I have.

LINCOLNSHIRE ECHO   Wednesday, October 21, 1987

● Sold for £150   Barrymore Halpenny (right) hands over his bottle of wine , bought by Norbert Stumm. Centre is Echo circulation manager, Bill Kennoway

LINCOLN wine merchant Norbert Stumm has given a double boost to the Echo's £65,000 Mencap appeal.

Not only has he handed over £150 for a bottle of vintage Montepulciano d'Abruzzo donated to the appeal by author Barrymore Halpenny, but he has come up with an idea for un-corking the mystery of the bottle and raising more money for Mencap at the same time.

Mr Stumm said he was satisfied the bottle con-tained a "beautiful" wine which it would be quite an experience to sample.

Now he is going to give interested wine con-noisseurs the opportunity to do just that — on con-dition that they make a donation to Mencap.

Mr Stumm said he planned to re-donate the bottle at the opening of the Mencap day centre on

Norbert shares his £150 wine

Tentercroft Street, which is the focus of the appeal.

People who were curious about the wine could then give money for the chance to sample it he said.

Mr Stumm said the bottle contained one of the finest

Italian wines. To give tasters an extra luxury, he promised to donate a top French wine — Chateau Mouton Rothchild 1979, worth £80 — to be sampled alongside it.

Work on the centre is due to be completed around the middle of next year Money raised from the tasting would go towards running costs, said Mr Stumm.

Mr Stumm said the wine had aroused a great deal of interest among his cus-tomers. He was sure many of them would be queuing up to taste it.

Page 192 – This shows my unique bottle of wine that I put to good use.

Page 193 – Top: A horse named Aaargh!

Page 193 – Bottom: The Author gives Aaargh! a lump of sugar. Note Aaargh poster on stable door. Aaargh did run at Doncaster, but not fast enough.

Page 194 – (above) Author in crew-room at RAF Wittering and poses for Station photograph during interview with the Italian Tornado pilot.

Page 195 – Keeping my word. I said only one bottle of wine a day and I will keep my word. Cheeeerrs.

196

Page 196 – Top: Having fun at the home of Winco Wallis. A handshake from my long-time friend to say he likes my ten-gallon Stetson hat that my son Baron had brought me back from the States.

Page 196 – Bottom: Ken now shows me his dance called the soft-shoe shuffle. Nifty footwork. You start with a sharp right turn with the right foot.

Page 197 – Top: At the Red Arrows, RAF Scampton with Eric Steenson and one time news reader Jan Leeming. A happy couple, it's what Eric Steenson said years later that makes me smile.

The last moments in 5 Squadron Crew Room at RAF Binbrook before it closed ... I and the sergeant were the last two before he locked up

Above left, a final cigar in 5 Squadron Crew Room
Above right and so, just one for the road. Photograph taken at my bar at home.

I end on a photograph of a control tower for many reasons, one being that they are symbolic of the airfields, but also due to the fact that back in the 1960's I sent to several magazines to take an article that I had done about our wartime airfields and in particular the history of our control towers. Many of these editors did not even bother to write back (and their magazines continued not to carry any articles like I was proposing), but one editor did reply ... he sent my own letter back to me and written on it was ... *"no one wants to read about old airfields, the war's over!"*

Over and quickly forgotten as were the memories of those that gave their all. Now you can understand the restless spirits. I don't forget them and I ensure through my work that they and their valiant deeds are never forgotten. Today things are to a certain extent better than when those breeds of editors ruled, but the same apathy exists.

COPYRIGHT AND WARNING NOTICE

GHOST STATIONS™

by
Bruce Barrymore Halpenny

The new series based on the original:

GHOST STATIONS™ 1
True Ghost Stories   (ISBN 978-1-871448-10-8)

GHOST STATIONS™ 2
True Ghost Stories   (ISBN 978-1-871448-11-5)

GHOST STATIONS™ 3
True Ghost Stories   (ISBN 978-1-871448-12-2)

GHOST STATIONS™ 4
True Ghost Stories   (ISBN 978-1-871448-13-9)

GHOST STATIONS™ 5
True Ghost Stories   (ISBN 978-1-871448-14-6)

GHOST STATIONS™ MYSTERIES
True Mystery Stories   (ISBN 978-1-871448-08-5)

GHOST STATIONS™ LINCOLNSHIRE
True Ghost – Mystery Stories   (ISBN 978-1-871448-06-1)

GHOST STATIONS™ YORKSHIRE
True Ghost – Mystery Stories   (ISBN 978-1-871448-05-4)

GHOST STATIONS™ GERMANY
True Ghost – Mystery Stories   (ISBN 978-1-871448-07-8)

GHOST STATIONS™ THE STORY
The Story about GHOST STATIONS™, featuring special stories, photographs and a glossary of the abbreviations used in the Series. The Story is a companion to the Series.

(ISBN 978-1-871448-09-2)

To keep up to date with books, news and general information regarding the one and only **GHOST STATIONS™** series, visit the official Website at:

www.ghoststations.com